Avril's Phoenix

Michelle Harris-Genge

Copyright © 2019 Five Crow Road Publishing Company. Cover design by Greg Webster Designs.

Five Crow Road Publishing Company
PO Box 274
Murray River PE
C0A1W0 Canada
fivecrowroad@gmail.com
www.fivecrowroad.com

ISBN: 978-1-9993957-2-8

DEDICATION

Avril's Phoenix is especially dedicated to Samuel Gordon Genge. You will forever be remembered and loved.

I also want to dedicate this novel to Geoff, Berry and Gideon. You make every single day lovely. I wouldn't want to be on this journey without you.

ACKNOWLEDGMENTS

First off, I would like to thank my friend Tracey MacIsaac. Tracey was the first person to read this book. She loved it, even though it was in the skeletal stages and (honestly) wasn't very good. Having this support was monumental in moving forward. I would also like to acknowledge Kirstin Lund's awesomeness. Kirstin was the first adult to whom I shyly admitted my desire to be a writer someday. She took me seriously and never told me that I was already grown up and shouldn't be so silly. I think she has read this book three different times (at least) and has provided excellent advice and editorial support throughout its journey. This novel has taken years to write and people have reviewed it at many, many stages. Providing critical feedback can be awkward and challenging. Sincere appreciation to everyone who read *Avril's Phoenix* and liked it, and extra credit to those who read it and told me what they didn't like about it. The book is better because of your feedback. I would like to thank everyone who has contributed to this process, including Shaun Edward-Smith, Michelle MacCallum, Emily Kierstead, Trisha Harris, Valerie Docherty, Patti Larson (especially Patti – you've been an eternally amazing mentor, advice-giver, reviewer and inspiration), Melissa Mullen, Kelly Buckley, and the PEI Writes Crew (Stacy, Kelly, Charity, Colleen, Julie, Kirstin, Patti – most of this book was written during our writing retreats. I can't express how important they are). Kudos to Greg Webster for another great cover. Thanks to Jane Ledwell for her exceptional editorial notes, and Tom Defusco for his fantastic copy edits. Last but not least, I would like to extend sincere gratitude to Susan Maynard who not only provided feedback, but eventually edited the final draft in full form. This book would not be the same without her excellent care and attention. If there are any mistakes left, it's because I messed up somehow.

CHAPTER 1

In my twelfth summer, the stark realization that innocence is fragile hit me like an undercut to my tiny chin. I learned quite young that life doesn't always desire to be subtle. The road less travelled isn't necessarily a choice. Sometimes life cuts you off, forcing you down a path that is dark and unwieldy. That summer, like all of the summers of my youth, my family stayed at my uncle's place for a couple of weeks. My mother's brother was a retired freighter captain who lived close to the ocean but inland enough that you could only smell the sea when it was really hot outside and the wind was blowing eastward. He still lived on the water, though, on a large glassy pond where he went fishing in the evenings.

The Captain didn't have any children but he tolerated us fairly well for someone who was used to no mess and a lot of quiet. Mom, Dad, the Captain and my aunt would gather around the fire pit in the evenings to discuss politics or other topics of no interest to kids. We had free rein in the mornings when all of the adults were sleeping in from the previous night's activities. My siblings would wake me up every morning at the break of dawn and we'd slip down the dewy lawn to the deck on the lake that had a swirly-slide mounted to its ledge. We would catapult off the slick, circular slide like a long line of maniacal penguins, electrifying our taut bodies as we hit the freezing water. One by one, we would pop up out of the lake, laughing, choking and screaming with joy. Over and over, we kicked and swam to the slide for another turn until we melted into the deck with sheer exhaustion, the smell of the sun-warmed cedar deck surrounding us like a comfortable blanket.

The Captain hired workers to make pathways around the property that were amply lined with edible treats – fruit trees we ate breakfast from, bushes we had dessert from, and berries with spiky vines that tripped us while they cut our arms and legs. As we got older and braver, we ditched the groomed trails for full-scale woods exploration. The property extended sixty acres in total so it was immense enough that if we ever ventured onto a neighbour's property, they never complained because no one was ever the wiser.

We also had access to all of the boats and kayaks that were otherwise locked in a fancy blue barn when we weren't around. The property came alive and started breathing when we were there. The land welcomed us as it gasped with exultation that someone finally relished and experienced its beauty instead of just looking at it through storm windows or a camera lens.

This is where my sister, my brothers and I truly bonded as a family. It was our haven. Other kids went to camp; we went to the Captain's. We didn't even mind that our friends weren't there to enjoy it with us because this was *our time*. Something inside of us knew this was precious. Just around the bend, we'd be doing separate things with different people when we ultimately grew up.

One Saturday morning when my siblings were uncharacteristically sleeping in, I slipped out of my bed and went down to the dock. I wasn't sure if I wanted to paddle or kayak, but in the end I chose the rowboat for a leisurely solo adventure. I loved the sound the oars made on the pond while they splashed in the water against the brisk morning light. I remember the boat was red with white trim. When I rowed, I could envision a shadow of pink on the water, like someone spilled a drop of oil paint on a glossy, wet canvas. I rowed out far enough so that the boat was close to the clay road bordering the Captain's property. I imagined how lovely it would be to get lost down the dirt road before gradually sauntering back to civilization. A couple of trucks drove by, but none stopped to appreciate the view. I was happy because I enjoyed my solitude. I didn't feel like making conversation with strangers, even if they were friendly ones.

I noticed something hovering on the cusp of the water a few feet away from the last of the weeds. I rowed closer and saw a black garbage bag. At first, I didn't think too much of it. I wasn't even being adventurous when I put my oar underneath it. I didn't really care what was in it. I was just traveling beside it, so I touched it. But then, because I had already made contact, I started to become interested in the guts of the bag. I fiddled around with it until the top of the bag unfastened and the contents rolled over the bottom of my oar. I screamed, then immediately shut my mouth because the foul stench of partially furred, decomposing kittens hit me like a savage punch to my face. I started rowing back at a frenzied, uncoordinated pace to get away from the smell and the sight. I stopped around fifteen feet away then watched, frozen, as the bag started to take on water and unceremoniously dropped to the bottom of the pond.

I returned a different person than the girl who began her trek that morning. By the time I got back to the Captain's, my siblings were awake and ready for the next adventure. I said nothing about the kittens because I didn't want to ruin anyone's day or bother the cranky adults. I think I told my sister years later, over margaritas. But by then it wasn't as monumentally tragic as it was the moment I realized reality can quickly switch when life haphazardly leaves baggage for others - even children - to deal with. And unfortunately, there were children like me who weren't able to deal with the weight, even after we became adults.

CHAPTER 2

I grew up with a set of twins and a sister. My mother had two babes for each of her arms – Joanie and me on the left, Billy and Ronnie on the right. Joanie still lives close by, but the twins literally live on the other side of the world. They moved to Asia together, came back home to have a double wedding, and then moved back to the other end of the world with their new wives. The family is split like a global grade-school dance: girls to the left of the earth, boys to the right. The absence of my brothers makes Mom's arms ache.

The twins grew into men called William and Ronald. I connect with them here and there, but it has been so many years since we've physically been together that we've lost touch. The link of childhood doesn't last forever, plus the sibling bond gets frayed when the time span between visits is too long. On their sporadic vacations, the twins still ruffle my hair when they pass by me in Mom's hallway, but it feels forced. It has become the touch of a wraith instead of the warm connection of family.

My brothers each have children and we are sent updates of their pictures. When they come home every couple of years, I see the children getting taller and more (or less) articulate. I try to deeply love my nieces and nephews, but my emotional DNA feels a bit detached. They seem like lovely people, but I don't know them well enough to know for sure. I give each of them hugs when they come to visit. We eat food together while they're here and we share popcorn if we have a family movie night. I miss them when they go, but I don't *love* them like I feel I should. It's more like a feeling of endearment. In the end, I just feel guilty because I'm not the auntie I was born to be.

I'm quite close with Joanie, though. Maybe too close sometimes. There are numerous moments when I want her to back off a bit. Even though I'm getting wrinkles from age, she still treats me like I'm a fifteen year old in need of protection. She is my knight in shining armor, even if I'm not a damsel in distress. She comes for dinner with Orrie, Duet and me every week or so. I love having her over, but there are many moments when she imposes a therapy session on me that I don't want or need.

I'm not bored with my life, Joanie ... I don't want to have a career right now ... Orrie isn't smothering my creative drive ... I do feel fulfilled ... Thanks, but I don't need to join your book club ... Yes, I still adhere to feminist philosophy, and while I understand your concern that I gave up my financial power to be a full-time mom, I don't really see it the same way ... I'm good ...

I want a lot of kids. Currently, we just have Duet, but both Orrie and I want a big family now that his law practice is going well. I can't wait. I just know things will be different with my new brood than they are with Joanie, Billy, Ronnie, and me.

My children will all get along famously. No geographical chasms will wreak havoc on my clan.

It will all come together flawlessly.

CHAPTER 3

"More wine?" Joanie asks.

"One alcoholic drink at lunchtime is my limit, thanks."

"Ah, the boundaries one has when others are in her care," Joanie gently chides as she orders another dark rum and diet cola.

"Nope, just being a responsible adult," I retort.

"What are you doing on Saturday?"

"I'm not sure. Orrie is off this weekend, or I guess I should say he's not putting in any overtime. We might go to a movie. Want to join?"

Joanie's ice cubes clink together as she swishes down the last of her beverage. "Thanks for the offer, but some friends are coming over and we're going to a fringe festival downtown."

"Sounds fun."

"Keeps the boredom at bay," Joanie mutters nonchalantly while she stirs her next drink.

I bike home in the sunshine, feeling relieved that I can make it up the hills better and better each day. I'm finally getting in shape. I tend to blame my figure on my previous pregnancy, but Duet was born four years ago, so this excuse really hasn't cut it for a while. I used to bike all the time when I was a kid, but for some reason I became extremely lazy after entering adulthood. My body is so relieved to be cycling again. The breeze caresses the sweat on my face while the hot sunshine massages my back as I zip through the streets.

I get home and throw my shoes into a pile with the other footwear. Orrie comes over quietly, his finger to his lips. "Shhh," he whispers. "The princess has worn herself out and is having a nap on the couch. Don't wake her."

"Okay," I whisper back. "What do you feel like doing? What can we do that's quiet?"

Orrie takes my hand and leads me to our bedroom. "I'm not promising it will be quiet, but I can think of something we can do while we have some alone-time."

"What if Duet wakes up?"

"She won't. I promise."

"How do you know?"

"I just do. Don't worry - everything will be okay. Trust me."

I giggle while following him to the room, but then have second thoughts once we get there. I finished up a batch of homemade wine a couple of weeks ago and we were quite frisky as we sampled the bottles. It was worth the mild hangovers, but it got me into trouble in the nether-region. I went to the doctor to check out what all of the irritation was about, and he told me I had honeymoon cystitis. I blushed, telling him I've been married for a long time. He teased that it's a good thing we're still in the honeymoon phase. He handed me a couple of prescriptions for antibiotics plus pills to dull the burning sensation. I've been taking the medication for a couple of days and am starting to feel better. One of the pills makes my pee a bright orange, which is a bit shocking to see, even though the information packet very clearly described this possibility.

"I'll need to take a rain check on your offer. I'm not feeling 100%."

"Oh, right. I forgot." Orrie frowns then snickers, "Orange pee killing the mood?"

"Ugh, I suppose so. Besides, Duet is going to a birthday party today, so I better get her up soon. It's at the local pool and I don't want to take any chances. A urinary tract infection plus a wet bathing suit don't jive at all."

"I'll take your word on that."

"Did you want to come, too? I don't really know anyone there; it's for Arnold's daughter."

"Arnold from accounting at the office?"

"Yes, I'm not sure why we were invited."

"Networking, I guess."

"So Duet and I are responsible for your networking?"

Orrie salutes me. "You are duty bound."

I take Duet to the party, awkwardly trying to socialize but no one is interested in engaging with me. I desperately need a wingman. Or a wingwoman. Without social supports, I skulk around the other moms, clumsily trying to infuse myself into conversations. Finally, I give up. I eat lots of cheese and cracker combos until my mouth is full so I can't talk. I nod and grin at conversations I'm not a part of, until I decide enough is enough and go in the pool with Duet. She's not Miss Popularity either. No one really notices that the two of us are playing together instead of with everyone else.

Duet loves it when I twirl her around the water. We're busy circling around the pool when I get an overwhelming urge to pee. I tell Duet we need to go in for a bit. As I'm walking through the water, I see a swish of fluorescent orange escape around my body. I look down in horror and then simultaneously dart my eyes around to the partygoers while ferociously splashing the water around to dissipate the evidence. I jump up and down and twirl Duet around to the point that she has never had so much fun in all her young life. I then panic and tone it down a bit, as I'm probably attracting unwanted attention. I look down at the water again for traces of orange, but I think I'm okay. One of the mothers is looking at me suspiciously though, so I'm not sure if I'm in the clear. I'm never going to ask, so I'll never know. I'm just going to pray I'll not be known as the mother who pees weird colors in the pool. Duet would never get invited to future birthday parties.

I gather Duet and the two of us have a shower. Afterwards, I try even harder to talk to all of the moms, mostly to try to gauge if they are judging me. It's as painfully awkward as it was before, so I can't really tell if they know or not. I want to tell them. I need them to know I didn't *mean* to pee in the pool, a bit just squirted out. I'm not gross - I just have a bacterial infection from having too much sex so I'm on a medication that makes my pee the color of rancid orange juice.

That's all.

CHAPTER 4

Bedtime is a big cozy blanket that pleasantly covers me for eight or nine hours every night. I cherish the opportunity to snuggle with Orrie or Duet in either of our beds. I even find myself sometimes aching for that specific comfort during the waking hours. Cuddling is my jam. It's an opportunity to simultaneously connect with my family, both physiologically as well as emotionally, and that linkage gets hardier the longer we cuddle. Bonds are created on a metaphysical level while we move around for comfort, dancing in the sheets for the best position for ourselves and each other.

I also love my prayer time with Duet at night. Just Duet, God and me. I feel closer to God when I pray with Duet than I do in any church on Sunday. It's sacred. We cuddle (of course) and I smell her hair, relishing the squeaky voice reciting the prayer I learned when I was a kid. It was a prayer that was written on a picture in my bedroom growing up. I think someone cross-stitched it for Mom as a baby shower gift when Joanie was born. I can still see it against the pink-checkered wallpaper on the left hand side of my bed. I also remember I used to take the picture down and put it under my dresser any time Joanie's friends blew cigarette smoke out the bedroom window when Mom wasn't home. I would even wash the blank space on the wall before I put it back up, after all the irreverent behavior. Even though I had a vague inkling God saw all, I didn't want my picture to see. The cross-stitched girl in the picture even looked a bit like Duet, all bouncy - yet respectful - as she asked God to protect her.

Now I lie with Duet as she prays, sometimes into the pillow, sometimes with both of her hands clasped tightly while sitting upright next to me. While she's praying, I send up a word of thanks for this gift I have lying beside me. There is nothing more precious than your child. I look down at Duet and pray that all my future children will be as amazing as her. *Dear God, let the stars align again.* As I lie next to Duet, I gently pat my stomach.

There's
something
going
on
in
my
belly.

I feel something quirky happening inside my gut, and female intuition tells me it's not gas. There's no movement, necessarily, just an alien sensation within. I don't believe an extra-terrestrial has hijacked my body, so I think I might be pregnant. I've been feeling a bit sick lately, as if my body is rejecting something that normally isn't there. I never had morning sickness with Duet, though, so I might just be imagining things.

When can you take a pregnancy test? I think I remember from a television commercial that you can find out in as little as a week. When should I pee on the stick? I bought a test six months ago and it turned out negative, so maybe my female intuition is wishful thinking. Still, the tests are cheap enough, so I might as well buy one. It was pretty depressing last time, though. I slowly waited an eternity for the positive sign to appear, but it never happened. I sat on the toilet for a good ten minutes, thinking my urine was a late bloomer and it would turn pink any second, but it never did. Orrie was waiting outside the bathroom door telling me to get off the pot and everything will be okay.

"We can try again – it will be fun," Orrie said.

"Yeah, I know," I replied. "I'm just a little disappointed."

"Do you want to get started now?" he joked.

"Nah, I'm okay. Thanks, though."

Maybe this time I won't tell him I'm taking a test. That way if it turns out negative he won't have to feel like he needs to comfort me. Sometimes you just want to feel sad without the bother of other people trying to make everything all right.

I lay my hand on my abdomen, rubbing it. "Are you there?" I mumble.

"Who you whispering to, Mommy?"

"No one, sweetie."

"Yes, you are. I can hear you. Are you talking to Webster?" Webster is Duet's imaginary friend. Or at least I assume he's imaginary. Maybe he's a ghost I can't see because I'm too old. They say kids can see angels too.

I don't respond quickly enough. "So who?" Duet pushes.

"I'm just talking to my belly."

"Why? Does it hurt?"

"No."

"So why, then?"

"Because it was in the mood for conversation."

"Is it lonely?"

"I hope not. I hope it feels loved."

"I love my belly," Duet declares, patting her protruding stomach. Kids have the best bellies. They just let them hang out with no shame or care. It's awesome. Actually, it's just like a pregnant woman's belly. I look at Duet's stomach, comparing it to mine. She definitely has more of a pot than me. I wonder how long it will take before I start to show.

"What are you thinking about, Mommy?"

"I'm just thinking about how much I love you."

"I love you too," she chirps before returning to her prayers.

I've been deliriously happy for the past four years she's been in my life. I never want her to feel the pressure of my love, though. I don't want to burden her with a needy mother who won't let her child grow up and move away. But if I were to be brutally honest with myself, I would like her to move away for a very short snippet and then come back home after she gained the necessary wisdom to determine that she's happier to be within walking distance from me. Will I feel the same way about you, Belly? When will you start to take on your own identity? It's going to be so much fun having a couple of kids around the house. We can convert the den into a nursery – it's going to be such a blast.

No … don't jinx it. Best not to think about nurseries and the like until I take a test and my belly is validated. I want to tell the whole world you're coming, Belly, yet I'm terrified to let anyone know because you might not be. If I find out I'm not pregnant, what is that? It's not like I lost you because you never were. How does that work? Is it a type of emotional miscarriage?

Okay, enough.

I just need to confirm I'm pregnant and then everything will be all right and I'll stop worrying about something that will never, ever happen.

CHAPTER 5

There's a line.

There's a pink line right where it said there would be.
There's a pink line right where it said there would be if I'm
pregnant.
There's a pink line right where it said there would be if I'm
pregnant so that means
that
I'm
pregnant.

I'm pregnant.
There's a line.

CHAPTER 6

Joanie is away on a trip for work, so I'm forced to have this conversation over the phone. The first time I try to call, there's a lot of music in the background so I assume she's in a bar. I tell her I'll call her later. I wait five minutes and give her another call. By this time, she is on the way to her hotel room. Joanie tells me she'll call back when she gets there. It must have been a pretty boring hotel bar if she was geared up to leave it so easily.

The phone rings and I answer it quickly - both because I'm excited to talk to her, but more so because I don't want to wake Duet. I'm huddled in the corner of Orrie's office. I don't normally come in here, even though I have my own pretend desk in the corner. Orrie didn't want me to feel like I'd given up my connection to the professional world, so he gave me half his career space in the household. I sit at the comfy chair by his desk while I talk to Joanie.

"So, what's up?" Joanie asks.

"I'm pregnant."

"Wow, that's awesome!" she gleefully shouts. I suspect her happiness is enhanced by a couple of cocktails.

I take a breath to prepare for my confession. "I haven't told Orrie yet."

"Why on earth not?"

"I'm not sure. I know he'll be pleased. I just don't know. I feel shy about it for some reason. That's weird, right? I'm being weird."

"What? You've been married forever. You have a kid together, he saw you give birth. He's probably seen you on the toilet. What's left to be shy about?"

"I know. It's odd. But I never told him I took a pregnancy test, so now everything is awkward. And no, he's never seen me on the toilet. Gross." I shift the phone to my other ear. "How are your meetings going?"

"Pretty good. Networking and such, you know. But I don't really understand why you haven't told Orrie."

"I know, I know. I don't even understand it myself. Why wouldn't I?"

"He wants another baby, doesn't he?"

"Of course."

"Then I don't get it."

"I just don't know how to tell him. It's so big. It's a huge life-altering event that's here all of a sudden."

"How did you do it with Duet?"

"Don't you remember? You let it slip that Orrie was planning a surprise birthday party for me, so I told him I thought I was pregnant. We celebrated with a pregnancy test instead. There was a bottle of expensive wine at the ready in case it was negative, so it was a win-win scenario."

"Did you guys ever have that wine?"

"Yeah, about a year ago."

"So why did you take the test without him this time?"

"I wanted to be alone if it ended up I wasn't pregnant. I didn't want it to be a big deal."

"Will he be upset you took it without him? Is that why you're worried?"

I twirl around in the office chair. "I'm not worried. I just don't know how to tell him. I'm really happy about this, but it's so big. I don't know how to handle it, you know? Does that make sense? Am I being really strange?" I stand up to stretch my legs. "I'm so excited to tell him, I might burst when the words are coming out."

"Don't overanalyze it. It's easy. You just ... oh wait, someone's knocking at my door. Just a sec, I'm going to look through the peep-hole."

"Did you order room service?" I sigh nostalgically. "I miss room service."

"No," she answers as she moves with her phone. I hear a metal clink as she checks to see who's there. "Oh, Avie? Can I give you a call tomorrow?"

"Why? Do you have a male visitor?"

"Yes."

"Someone serious?"

"No, he's just someone I would like to hang out with tonight."

"Okay. Have fun," I say, as I am about to hang up.

"Avie? I'm so thrilled for you. Seriously. I'm totally ecstatic, and I know Orrie will be too."

I smile. "Love you, JJ."

"Love you, baby sister. Thanks for calling. You made my night. Give Duet a kiss without waking her. I'll see you soon."

I hang up the phone and head to the living room. Orrie will be home soon, and I can't wait to share my surprise. I just needed a tester before the big event. I send a mental thank-you to Joanie, hoping her evening works out well. I know mine is going to be fantastic, and part of its success will be due to her.

CHAPTER 7

I made a doctor's appointment today. Or I guess I made a nurse's appointment. I don't think the doctor sees patients until they are more than three months along and I'm probably not that far up the ladder yet. I'm only on the second rung, most likely. Someone is probably going to need to check the size of my uterus because I have no real idea when my last period was. I usually try to keep a mental tab on the dates but I guess I haven't been stellar at it lately.

This probably isn't something you want to know about, Belly – my period and such. Then again, right now you are a mass within me so you're completely comfortable with my bodily juices. Right now I am you. We're one for a bit until you get further along. Then you'll become more you, and less me, until we become two physical beings.

So it begins.

I can't believe I love someone I don't know at all. I have no idea what your personality is yet, but I'm totally in love with you. I can't imagine loving anyone as much as your sister Duet. But other mothers tell me that love expands when you have more children. It's a metaphysical wonder that defies explanation. I don't love you as much as Duet yet. That sounds like such a hurtful and unmotherly thing to admit, but I don't mean it maliciously. It's simply true. Also, I'm scared if something goes wrong I won't get to meet you. Or maybe I'm not really pregnant at all. Maybe the test was wrong and I've been living in a false reality.

Maybe. What if.

What kind of mother do you think I am, Belly, talking about my worries all the time? Here I am having a conversation with my unborn child who knows nothing about the world and I'm rambling about fear. You must think I am the most maudlin creature in existence. Maybe I am. Actually, I don't think so. I think it's normal to be afraid about something so important. But that must freak you out too. Soon you are going to be entering a world where people are frightened all the time. Great. *Hello world, here I come – watch out! AAAH.*

It's not that bad. Well, yes it is, I guess. There's a lot to be terrified of out here. There's an eternal war brewing overhead. But there's counterbalance everywhere with so much that is utterly wonderful. I guess you epitomize this, Belly. I'm so worried about you, but you make me so utterly joyful that life just wouldn't be complete without you. I'm quite happy for the fear.

Bring it on, baby.

CHAPTER 8

The sermon today was perfect. It was just what I needed to hear. I know God will always protect me, but sometimes I just need to hear it out loud. Not that the Pastor necessarily framed his sermon this way, but that's what I took from it.

When I was growing up, my family went to church for all of the important holiday sermons – Christmas, Easter and the like. We would get dressed up, the twins would fight with Joanie and me in the back seat the entire trip there, and Dad would yell at everyone to behave like normal people. Mom would tell him this is exactly how normal people behave. *"We're not going to church because we're perfect, dear. We're going to church because we aren't. No one is."* We would sit as close to the back as possible, but not too far back that we would be judged. Plus, it was important to be seen. That was the whole point of going.

I never really thought about God as anything outside of an abstract obligation before I met Orrie. He grew up in a religious household, but I didn't even know he was a Christian until we became close friends in university. He was more of the quietly converted type. I know he would have loved and married me even if I remained an ambivalent believer, but over the years, I was gently swayed through his perseverance and unswaying faith in God. Even when his parents died, he didn't balk. It only helped him along, knowing they were "in a better place."

I enjoy going to church now. It almost feels rebellious lately. It seems like in the past, people went to church because that's what you were supposed to do. Nowadays, going to church makes you suspect. People are at the ready with judgment, waiting for you to be judgmental first. Most of our friends are polite and don't voice anything, but I can see suspicions wafting across their foreheads, wondering why seemingly smart people believe in such notions of death and redemption.

After today's church service, we go to a nearby restaurant to order brunch. Once we're seated, the waitress brings over crayons so Duet can scribble on her placemat. Orrie and Duet have a couple games of Xs and Os while I chat with some friends at another table. Orrie orders for me before I get back. I don't say anything, even though it annoys me that he orders waffles when I wanted an omelet.

Orrie hands me a napkin. "Anything up this week?"

"My calendar is filled with playgroups and appointments," I smirk. "Monumental stuff. You?"

"I shouldn't be late too often this week."

"That's good. It's nice to have you around in the evenings. It gets my mind off my mind."

Orrie's forehead wrinkles. "Everything okay?"

"Of course, I just like having you around. What could go wrong?"

CHAPTER 9

Okay.

Tomorrow is D-day. Doctor day.

Tomorrow I find out for sure what's going on in my abdomen. I will be able to concretely ascertain how long Belly has been a member of my body. I hope it's a minimum of three months. This would mean we get to tell everyone. It's so hard to live with this secret.

"Wine, Avril?"

"No, thank you."

"Oh. Why? Not feeling well?"

"No, I guess not. Thanks, though."

And then Orrie proceeds to consume as much liquor as he wants. It's not fair that men have a completely different role in pregnancy. They can choose how far they go in the whole procedure. And everyone applauds when they are fully engaged.

"Oh, look at that. Orrie hasn't had a beer since he found out Avril was pregnant. Isn't that sweet! He's going to be such a wonderful father..."

Whereas, if I were to have a wine, it would be:

"Oh, look at that. She's pregnant and she's drinking. What kind of a mother is she going to be? No wonder the world is in such a state, hmm? Someone should call Child Protection..."

In all honesty, I have no desire to have any wine or anything else that could potentially be damaging to my baby's health. I sincerely want a happy tenant, and I'm so eager to have Belly around that I don't mind the minor inconveniences. But sometimes (sometimes) I get a little jealous of Orrie's ability to do whatever the heck he wants because no one is ingesting his fluids on a continual basis. Sometimes (sometimes) I wish it was a literal shared pregnancy, where I could take some breaks here and there to have a coffee with some chocolate-covered coffee beans, while gulping a double espresso.

Just (sometimes).

Barring my annoyance with the gender inequities of pregnancy, I'm quite excited about tomorrow's appointment. I can't feel Belly yet when I put my hands on my stomach. The baby isn't moving around, as far as I can tell. So far he/she is just making me nauseated and constipated. I lie down on the bed, trying to get a grip but there's only a tiny bulge that could just as easily be my bladder, or gas, or a lot of pepperoni pizza with fast-rising crust. I can't wait until the doctor tells me the arrival date. It's like she will legitimize the birth. Belly isn't real until someone tells me so.

What does this disclose about me? Shouldn't I be completely in tune with my body? Especially now? Did I know with Duet? I think so, but I can't remember. I can't even remember a monumental event in the birth of my firstborn child – an epic event in my life. I think I'm a good mother, though. I might not have the best memory, but I do remember I loved Duet even before she was born and I love Belly now. I just need the doctor to tell me he or she is really coming. Then I'll love him or her even more.

CHAPTER 10

Gynecological exams are a real blast. I think I might prefer rolling around in glass and pouring lemon juice all over the cuts, but this poses strong competition. I arrive early for my appointment because it's frowned upon if you arrive late. I then wait 45 minutes past my allotted time before I go in to get weighed and get my blood pressure taken, and all of the other precursor measures before the big exam. I've gained another four pounds since last week. I have no idea how ... I might be binging just the tiniest bit on desserts lately but nothing that substantial. I explain this to the nurse. She really doesn't care.

"Just as long as you're gaining, dear," she mumbles distractedly.

There's another woman in the chair beside me getting her blood pressure taken. She's about my size – maybe a bit smaller – but comparable. I imagine she's around twenty weeks at the most. I cheerfully catch her eye. "So how far along are you?"

"Oh, I think I am at my 37th week," she beams smugly. "I keep losing track with this one. I even knew how many days I was with my first child." She nods to a beautiful little blond cherub beside her.

I smile at her while telling myself she is an undernourished, bad mother for not gaining enough weight. Somehow it makes me feel better to think she's doing something wrong for looking so fantastic. I don't even feel guilty for feeling that way. I blame my irrational behavior on nasty hormones. I have to admit, I love the hormone factor. I have raging hormones so if I feel like being a raving lunatic when Orrie doesn't do the dishes for the umpteenth time, I freely freak out. I don't have to be nice all the time. I'm too tired to be sweet. If I can't find a clean spoon, I can yell as loud as I want and there's nothing anyone can do about it. It's very liberating. Maybe I'll yell at the nurse for making me gain four pounds.

Just before I start my verbal rampage, the nurse comes around the corner, sweetly telling me to follow her to the exam room. I'll wait until next month to let loose. I just don't feel right doing so when she's smiling at me with a toothy grin.

Ten minutes later, I'm back to hating my nurse with a guilty fervor. I am not a patient patient. I have no idea why you leave the waiting room so you can wait in another room. It doesn't make sense. There must have been a psychological study at some point determining people were happier if they just got to move around. People don't mind waiting as much if they feel like they're getting somewhere. It's like putting mirrors in elevators to distract you from the fact you are in a claustrophobic space catapulting up and down with mere cables hanging you in space.

I wait, reading a different ancient magazine. I was told to strip down to just the hospital gown but I don't think they'll mind my socks. I would have taken them off, except I have an ugly callous on my toe. I don't feel like subjecting the doctor to it. Plus, my legs are hairy. Note to self: pedicure + shave necessary before next appointment.

I have no idea why these things would bother me when I am apparently comfortable with this woman looking into my vagina. I don't even know what it looks like myself. I took a mirror after Duet was born to see what the source of all my pain was about. I remember thinking it wasn't very pretty. I hope it looks healthier now. I was very swollen *down there* at the time, so I attribute the unpleasant viewing to that. I'll have to check it out again sometime to compare. I wonder if the doctor ever thinks about it. I can't see her *not* thinking about it – you'd have to imagine there would be a little bit of patient comparison happening, if just on an intellectual level. *"My 10:00 vulva is just lovely. No freckles and everything is perfectly proportionate. My 11:00, on the other hand, is simply awful. I don't know how that woman can even pee..."*

Best not to think about it.

I'm in the middle of consciously not thinking about it when the doctor comes in. We go over the fluctuating temperatures outside, my last birth, a few questions about my diet and then the moment arrives. I get internally prodded, yet heroically continue my conversation about the nasty weather with her. *"Yes, it's been quite cold outside lately ..."* We talk about Duet and how she's coming along. We basically talk about anything that doesn't involve the procedure at hand. I wonder if this is a medical school course - Convo 101: Passing time when your hands are in otherwise inappropriate places. The time finally comes when she checks out my uterus to determine the approximate age of the baby. I tell her I think I had a period a couple of months ago, but none since then. I have no idea if I had my last period at the beginning or end of the month in question. Even so, she tells me I'm probably around eight weeks along. Which is impossible. I must be around three months or so. I have to be. I want to tell people about the event. There's no way I can wait another month before I start spreading the news.

"Is there any way I can be around twelve months?"

The doctor laughs. "Twelve months? I don't think so."

"Twelve weeks, I mean. Could I be around three months along?"

"Do you want to start telling people?"

"Yeah," I sheepishly admit. My cheeks start to turn red. I fleetingly wonder if other parts of your body turn color when you're embarrassed.

"Well, it's only recommended you wait out the three months because the chances of something going wrong are smaller, but it's completely your discretion if you choose to tell people before that. It's not like there are any hard-core rules. You're young and healthy, and your last pregnancy went well. You don't have any history of miscarriages, either."

"Yeah, I know," I mutter. I am a good mother. I am a good pregnant mother. I eat all suggested servings of fruit every day and adhere to the other food groups as well. I get my rest; I do yoga. I do Kegel exercises like nobody's business. I can start to tell people. Even so, I politely tell the doctor I think she might be a bit off. She tells me it's not an exact date so we won't know until the ultrasound. Until then, we'll (she'll) assume I'm at the eighth week of term. The doctor exits the room, whisking off to the next uterus. Thankfully, I'm busy thinking of something else so I don't needlessly bother to ponder what the next lady-parts will look like compared to mine.

CHAPTER 11

I'm in a place Dante would have written about if he were a woman. I want to tell the world I'm not gaining weight superfluously. There's a reason behind the pudge. My butt isn't getting bigger because I've stopped going to the gym. I'm growing a new human inside of me, so I deserve to have a piece of cheesecake when the time is right to do so. It bugs me that all of the pregnancy books or websites I've read tell me I shouldn't start gaining weight until my fourth month. Who writes these articles anyway? Men? Models? Track stars? I started gaining the moment I peed on the stick. I honestly think I stepped from the toilet a whole three pounds bigger once I saw the pink stripe.

I'm gaining more weight this time than I did with Duet. I'm five years older and less stretchy. I totally think I'd be cool with the chubbiness *if I could just tell people I was pregnant.* Then I'd be blossoming and radiant. Now I'm just fat and oily. It's just another infernal week and a half until I get out my megaphone to start telling strangers on the street that Duet is going to have a little brother or sister to play with.

Orrie feels if it's such a big deal (telling people, not the birth itself) then we should just verbally bust loose. He isn't as anal as I am with dates and rules. I used to be more rebellious. I used to play around the rules, but now I'm a mother and I don't have that right or privilege. I'm the arbiter of regulations, not the flouter of them. I recognize I have challenges with the dichotomy of being both a mother and a woman. Before having a baby, it would have been fully legitimate to sneak sex with Orrie in public spaces where we could get caught. Now I sometimes feel odd just having sex in private. It took me forever to let him touch my boobs after breastfeeding Duet. It just felt so *dirty.* Not naughty, but downright dirty and wrong. My body was somehow transformed to a vessel for procreation and sustenance of others, not one that was so selfish to be sexual and vibrant. I have turned into a married spinster. Well, except when wine is involved. Then momma can come out to play.

I also attribute my rigid need for regulations to my father. He was a police officer who was all about the rules. It went well for him until he quit the force to become a born again hippie. He left my mom and didn't see the need to be bothered with his offspring. I don't even know which continent he lives on now.

I had panic attacks for a bit after Dad left. Maybe all of us did. I remember Mom looking like a fish out of water, eternally sucking in her cheeks and staring wide-eyed. She went from being a cheery part-time employee to an exhausted double-shift worker. It was like we had two ghosts for parents, one who only emotionally haunted us and the other who physically walked the hallways late at night, checking in on us kids to ensure we were still there.

Dad left us without any financial support. Mom needed to ensure we were fed and clothed, so she worked at least fifty hours a week in a variety of jobs. Mom didn't have a 'proper' education, so the only employment she could get was low pay and unsecure. She worked in donut shops during the day and cheap restaurants at night. We grew up quickly after Dad left because his leaving meant Mom was gone too. Joanie and I were old enough to take care of the twins. We looked after them until they escaped to afterschool sports where they could be raised by their coaches instead of their sisters. At least this way, they had a male influence in their lives.

We also became *that family* everyone talked about. Everyone knew our Dad left. Everyone knew the circumstances. We went from being normal to being pitied. That's the year Joanie started smoking in the school bathrooms, and I started pretending to be perfect to keep the anxiety at bay. The more rigid I became, the easier it was to breathe. I was at the top of each of my classes and took part in whatever extra-curricular activity my teachers suggested. I kept busy as a bee so the humming would block out the questions. *Did Dad leave because of me? Does he have a new family? Were we the practice round before he found the right kids to love and cherish?*

I also started working part-time jobs as soon as I was legally able. I was never going to be financially dependent on anyone. Ever. If anyone ever left me again, I was going to be prepared. It wasn't until a year or so into my stay-at-home parenting stint with Duet that I realized I was betraying my younger resolve. Orrie saved me from the curse of abandonment. I know he will never leave me. I have nothing to worry about, so maybe I should stop being so rigid. Maybe it's time to take the yoke off my shoulders and relax. I need to stop being burdened by my past. My future is what I need to concentrate on. I don't need to be beholden to practices that don't truly protect me. It's finally safe to break loose. It is finally time to be free to tell everyone I'm pregnant, not fat.

CHAPTER 12

I can't breathe anymore. I lumber up two measly flights of stairs to Joanie's apartment and my lungs are under the impression I've participated in a marathon.

Stupid lungs. Stupid deluded organs.

Or I guess it's a single organ, isn't it? People say lungs, but it's not really two lungs. Or is it? There's your left lung and your right lung, so it would be organs not organ. Or is it one organ with two parts? I'm not a doctor. I don't know such things.

Doesn't matter. Stupid body that isn't working properly. Stupid body that's tired all the time. Stupid bladder – all I want to do is have one ferocious burst of urine and be done with it. Why do I have to go through the process of all these little squirts here and there, running out of breath while I'm on my way to the washroom?

I take a break on the step, rubbing my abdomen. *Belly, I don't want you to think I'm blaming any of this on you. None of this is your fault, little one. It's my stupid, fat body that can't use its own resources to properly breathe and pee.*

On the plus side, my pregnancy is going quite well overall. I'm not throwing up all the time. That's a definite bonus, for sure. Belly and I are copacetic. We meld well. It's like we're dancing partners in the process of creating life. Maybe that's why I'm so out of breath all the time – I'm dancing twenty-four hours a day. No wonder I'm tired. I apologize lungs, you're doing a great job. I'm still upset with my bladder, though. There's no logical explanation for your poor performance at all. Stupid organ. Or organs. Whatever. Stupid, stupid, stupid.

Joanie greets me at the door with a hug. "You look lovely, all glowing and shiny," she squeals.

"I'm sweating from exhaustion." I knead my knuckles along my lower back. "You, on the other hand, are gorgeous. I love your new hairstyle." I'm not giving undue compliments to be polite. Joanie looks fantastic. She always does, it comes as naturally to her as blinking. Or maybe it's all her expensive eye shadow. She is always made up to the max, even in the mornings. I think she even puts on makeup to buy milk. What would she ever do in a fire? Die in the bathroom while she fixes her face? I would be able to freely escape any inferno, as I never put on anything other than moisturizer. I tried mascara a couple of times, but it always ended in tears and black eyes. Lipstick sticks to my teeth, so it's a disaster on me too. If I wear blush, I look like I'm eternally embarrassed. It's just not my thing.

"Are you ready to go? I've wanted to see this movie forever, but I was patient." Joanie picks up a designer leather purse sitting on a chair by the door and casually swings it over her shoulder. "Did Mom call you? She wants to meet us there."

"Yes, I talked to her this morning. She's going to buy all the popcorn."

"She can't afford that, I hate when she does stuff like that." Joanie reaches past me to open the door and waits for me to exit.

"I know, but there isn't anything you can do about it. It's your fault for buying the tickets." I poke her shoulder with my index finger.

Joanie shrugs. "I figured if I bought all of them, she wouldn't feel targeted."

We try to meet up with Mom every month or so for excursions around the city. And each time, we try to find ways to sneakily purchase everything for Mom, but she's too smart to let us get away with it. Mom is living off a pretty meager income. Thankfully, the twins (or at least one of them) bought our family home from Mom as "an investment". I think she made arrangements to pay the monthly mortgage, or something along that line. Billy tried to fill me in the last time he was home, but we never had a chance to really get into it. I think he tried to get her to stay there for free, but she threatened to move to an apartment complex if he didn't take her money.

We get to the theater, giving Mom hugs before we go to our seats. I go to the bathroom a couple of times during the movie. Fortunately, I'm at the end of the aisle so I don't annoy anyone too much. The movie is enjoyable, nevertheless I'm okay with the multiple escapes to the washroom. I take my time because the movie has some creepy parts to it. I don't want Belly to experience anything scary. Also, the speakers are blasting so loudly I feel like it's physically moving the seats. I'm sure that would be jarring, as well. During one of the lulls in the movie when everything is peaceful, I rest my head on Mom's shoulder, catching a whiff of her perfume. I hope Belly is able to smell mom too. It's the same fragrance she's worn for decades, or maybe it's just how she naturally smells, her internal loveliness escaping in scented form. Either way, I sit contentedly in my seat, basking in mom's comforting aroma. I ignore the impending scary bits of the film, focusing on slowly breathing in, then breathing out.

Later that night, I tuck Duet in her bed and finish a couple of errands before heading upstairs. The house is toasty hot. I always turn up the thermostat on the nights I know Orrie is going to be working late. Ultimately, he ends up opening the window in our bedroom, but then we cuddle under the duvet, our noses cold while the rest of our bodies feel warm and cozy.

I go to the bedroom and turn on the TV to keep me company. I have all my lights on while I try on outfits to see what fits and what needs to be put away in storage. Fewer and fewer items remain in my closet. Even as I change clothes, I don't look in the mirror when I'm naked. I don't really want to see what I look like in all the lumpy, bumpy flesh. But then I get intrigued – what *do* I look like? I have stretch marks at all of the usual suspect locations, plus I'm ballooning out in my belly and butt. What does this all lead to? What is the total package?

I tiptoe out to Duet's room to ensure she's asleep, then go back to my room, gently closing the door. I look over at the window, noting the curtains are safely closed to block any unwitting viewers. I ruffle my bare feet in the carpet to start the strip. Pants go first; then underwear; then sweater, T-shirt and bra. I boldly stand in front of the full-length mirror, opening my eyes to focus full attention to my reflection.

Unfortunately, I'm not too far off from what I suspected I would see. Legs are more cellulite-y than before. I turn around. My bum has joined the party with my legs so they are all in a lumpy mess together. Known stretch marks are highly visible in the unfriendly lights. My boobs are huge, but not in a voluptuous way – more like a granny who took an air pump to herself inappropriately. I'm turning around in wonder and fascination, when I hear the bedroom door handle turning.

A robber! He's going to see me naked! How embarrassing!

I try to dart to the bed for cover, but it's too far away. I end up being clumsily mid-turn when Orrie enters the room. As I fall to the floor, I see the shock on his face. "Look away!" I yell. "Give me a second, would you? Why are you home? Can't you knock?" I spew at him in a torrent of garbled words.

I grab my big sweater from the floor, trying to cover myself but it doesn't even begin to hide the grotesque display. With as much dignity as I can muster, I crawl like a giant octopus over to the bed, ducking under the covers. "It's okay. You can look now," I groan with my eyes downcast.

Orrie's eyes are popped open as they dart around the room. "What are you doing?"

"What does it look like? I'm trying on clothes. Why didn't you knock? Can't a person have a bit of privacy in her own home?"

"Sorry, you usually leave all the lights on downstairs when you go to bed. I called for you when I came in. I figured you were asleep."

"I never sleep with the door shut. You know that. You should have knocked."

"But then I wouldn't have gotten to see you naked," Orrie crookedly smiles. "It's been awhile."

"I don't want you to," I pout.

"Why?"

"Because I look like what you saw."

"You look great. You look like you're having a baby. I love how you look."

"I look like a whale."

"You look like a woman. You look like what you're supposed to. Can I have another peek?"

I'm about to say no, but then I look at him, feeling shame about my shame. Why do I have to be so superficial and concerned about my body? Doesn't he love me for me?

"Okay," I agree, "but you need to turn off the lights and television. You can look at me in the shadows." I lift the covers for him and there are zero complaints about shapes or lumps or the room being too warm.

CHAPTER 13

"Engage!" I yell over to Duet as she runs towards me.

"Fire in the hole!" Orrie chimes in.

Our next-door neighbors walk by with their dogs, twisting their faces in contempt. *Why do they need to be so weird?* They wonder. *Why can't we just be surrounded by normal people?*

I don't care. I'm playing with Duet. When I am in mommy mode I'm not bothered by how others perceive me. I wish I was like this forever, but I'm only graced with it in small pockets of time and play. My normal self might cringe at the thought of my neighbors judging me. My mommy me couldn't give a sweet fig. I'm playing. I'm running around with my daughter while she laughs and snorts and loves life.

Orrie comes over, asking if we should take a break. He's tired and winded.

"You're an old man," I giggle, my breath coming out like smoke in the cold air. "Too many hours at the office wasting your muscles."

"I'm the same age as you, you just look better."

"Well, aren't you the sweet one? Whatever you want for a snack while we break is yours."

Duet overhears the opportunity for food and chimes in that she wants ice cream. She always wants ice cream. I love ice cream too, so I secretly use her desire as a vehicle to fulfill my cravings.

"Do you want to go for a walk up to the ice cream shop, or would you prefer if I made something at home? I don't think we have much variety, though. Maybe a bit of strawberry …"

"Are you steering me in the direction of going out to buy some?"

"Nope, just stating the facts, barrister."

Orrie grabs my hand, pulling me along. "Well, let's go then."

Life is perfect. Cue music.

CHAPTER 14

"I can't believe we've been waiting this long. I'm going to burst."

"Are you sure you can't go to the bathroom to pee a little bit?" Orrie asks. "Just enough so you'll stop complaining?"

"I'm not complaining; I'm literally about to explode. You've never had to do an ultrasound, so you have absolutely no idea what I'm going through. This is even worse than labor. I'm six months pregnant. I'm bursting. My bladder is going to slap you in the face once it explodes from my body from excess retention."

"I'm sure it isn't. And stop using the word 'literally' incorrectly."

"Oh, you're sure, are you? And you're mixing up your verb tenses."

"You know what I mean. And I'm not."

"I'm so uncomfortable."

"Well, I'm sure you can pee enough so you can sit properly."

"The brochure states you can't." I shift my position on the hard plastic chair.

Orrie gestures to the woman behind the desk. "Why don't you ask her?"

"She's a receptionist, not a nurse," I bite.

"I'm sure she'd know, though."

"Oh, you're sure, are you?" I say in the most sarcastic voice I can.

"Well, there's no reason to take it out on me. I'm sorry you're so uncomfortable."

"Sitting in a chair for too long is 'uncomfortable.' Having a cramp in your leg is 'uncomfortable.' Being in a state where, if I breathe wrong I'll urinate all over the place, is torture."

"If you're sure."

I look at him and we both start laughing. "Don't," I gasp, "I really will pee."

"Avril?" A woman in scrubs is standing with a chart at the entrance of the brightly lit hallway leading to the examining rooms.

"Yes, that's us. That's me," I correct myself.

"Can you follow me, please?"

I waddle down the corridor, grabbing Orrie's hand. "This is it," I smile.

"I wonder if he or she will look like Duet."

I squeeze Orrie's hand. "I hope so."

We get to the room and the nurse helps me on the bed. "Lie here and lift your shirt over your belly." She turns to Orrie. "Wait in the hall until the technician gives the okay."

"Can't he stay?" I ask.

"No, it's procedure. The father waits until the technician informs otherwise."

"Can she pee a little? She's really uncomfortable," Orrie asks the nurse.

"You can use the bathroom over there, but make sure you don't expel all of the urine."

"I guess I'll just wait. I don't want to get off the bed again."

She pats my knee, then turns out the light as she leaves.

The technician enters the darkened room. "Hello, Avril. How are you doing today? Excited?"

"Yes, very."

"Is this your first ultrasound?"

"No, I had one with my first baby."

"Well you know the process then," she mutters as she oozes gooey fluid all over my abdomen.

"The instrument is going to feel a bit cold. Let me know if you get uncomfortable."

"Okay," I nod as I close my eyes. A bit of cold fluid is nothing compared to my bladder's desire to let go all over the paper-covered cot. I pray I won't pee all over the bed. I stay still, staring at the ceiling while I listen to her clicking the machinery to input the data.

Her permanent smile disappears suddenly. "I'll be right back."

"Why, is something wrong?" A nervous flutter begins to grow in my chest. "I know I'm a couple of weeks late for my ultrasound. My husband had to go away for work so my daughter and I went with him ..."

She pinches her eyebrows together and then releases them, shaking her head. "I just have to get someone. I'll be right back."

"Is everything okay?"

She hesitates. "No, it's standard procedure. I just want my supervisor to see this."

"See what?" I try to sit up but it's too much work so I lay my head back on the paper-covered pillow.

"It's standard procedure," she repeats. "I'll be just a moment," she says as she goes through the door.

I wait for an eternity while my bladder berates me for making it go through this abuse. Around five minutes later two technicians enter the room. They do their clicking and inputting and the light from the monitor gives their faces an eerie, ghostlike glow. The supervisor looks at me and tells me it will all be over shortly.

"That's good," I say. "I can't wait to see the baby's picture. Can you tell if it's a boy or girl?"

The supervisor doesn't answer me right away. I'm ticked off at her rudeness. All she has to say is yes or no. "Are you sure nothing is wrong?"

They glance at the screen and then at each other. Finally, the supervisor looks at me. "Actually, Avril, there is," she softly conveys. There's something terribly wrong. I'm going to get your husband, okay? Wait right here."

My blood and brainwaves jump to attention. What? What did she say? What could be wrong? Where is she going to go? What?

What?

Orrie comes in the room, illuminated by the same evil green light as the technicians. I feel like I'm in a horror movie from the fifties before they had the ability to generate better special effects.

"What is wrong?" I assert, trying to muster maternal calmness, but my voice comes out squeaky and high pitched.

"Avril, there's a problem with your baby's spinal -"

"He won't be able to walk?" I interrupt.

"No, it's something more serious."

"He's completely paralyzed?" I ask. "Will you have to operate in utero?"

"No, I'm sorry. I called your doctor. She will be able to explain further. Your baby has no head."

"What do you mean?" Orrie demands, horrified.

"Your baby has what's called anencephaly. It's quite serious. Very, very serious."

I can't get any air into my lungs. "So what can you do? Is it life threatening?"

"You should go to your doctor for more information. I'm really sorry."

"Sorry? Sorry for what? What do you mean?"

"Your baby isn't going to survive. You should go to your doctor for more information. She's waiting for you."

"What's she going to do?"

"Come on, Avril. We better get going," Orrie quietly instructs as he tries to get me up.

"Orrie, what's going on? What's she saying to me? Is there something wrong with our baby?" I start crying.

The technician's assistant cocks her head to the side. "Would you like a couple of minutes to compose yourselves?"

"Avril, come on. Let's go," Orrie says in a daze. "We have to go."

"Where?"

"To the doctor's." He slips his arm under my shoulders and lifts me off the bed.

I feel like I'm someone else. "But there's nothing she can do."

"Come on, Avie. We have to go."

I slip off the table until my feet hit the floor with a thud.

"Do you want to go to the bathroom first?" the grim reaper asks.

"No, I'm okay."

Orrie takes my hands in his. "I think you should go to the bathroom, Avie," he whispers.

"I can't. I don't have to go anymore."

We travel in eerie, timeless silence downtown to our OB-GYN's office. Once we enter the waiting room, the nurse beelines over and directs us into one of the examining rooms without looking at us or saying a word.

"Was she smiling when she told us?" I ask Orrie.

"What, Avie?"

"The technician was smiling at us when she said our baby was going to die."

"I don't think she was smiling, Avie," Orrie mumbles.

"Yes, she was. She had a crocodile smile on. I saw her smiling. I know I did."

"I really don't think so, Avie." Orrie puts his face in his hands, pressing his fingers deeply into his temples.

"Where are we?"

He pulls his hands away from his face. "We're in the doctor's office."

"What's going on?" I cry.

"I don't know." Orrie's voice is dead. A tear rolls down his face, but he doesn't bother to wipe it.

"What's taking her so long? We've been here for ten minutes. What's she doing? Golfing? Talking to a friend on the phone?" I demand as I run towards the door. "I'm leaving."

Orrie grabs my shoulder. "Avie, come back. We have to stay until we know what's going on."

"I'm going to get the doctor," I grab the door knob.

"Just wait and I'll get the doctor. Just wait here, okay?" He gently moves my hand from the knob, replacing it with his own. He's about to leave when the doctor appears, counteracting his efforts to leave the room.

"What took you so long?" I quietly yell.

"Avril, I'm so sorry. I was just talking to the hospital about your appointment."

"What appointment?" Orrie backs into the room to stand beside me.

The doctor waves at two chairs beside the examining bed. "Sit down, please."

"I have to pee," I bawl.

"You go to the bathroom, this can wait."

"No, I don't need to." I sit down in one of the chairs.

The doctor looks at me like she is placating a child. "Are you sure? This can wait a few minutes."

"What's going on? Is there something wrong with my baby? How can there be something wrong with my baby? I'm six months along. Everything is supposed to be okay at this point."

Orrie comes over, kneeling beside my chair. "It's okay, Avie. Let the doctor talk."

"It's not okay, Orrie. What's she going to say?"

"I know this must be hard for you," the doctor starts.

"You don't know anything," I whimper.

"Go on, doctor." Orrie clamps his hand on my shoulder.

"I can only imagine how hard this is, but I really have to tell you the details. Your baby has a condition called anencephaly. At some point, probably around six weeks, there was a severance of the spinal cord. What this means is your baby's brain didn't develop properly."

"But he's kicking. I can feel him kicking right now." I point to my belly, trying to refute whatever she's trying to tell me.

"Yes, that's true. While the fetus is in the womb, it's fine because it's living off of you; but it won't be able to survive on its own. It's terminal. The baby will most likely be stillborn.

I've made an appointment at the hospital for you to go in next Tuesday. They'll induce you. You'll have a normal delivery."

"What do you mean?" Orrie jumps up from his crouch. "Tuesday is a couple of days away. How is she going to cope for that long?"

"He's kicking, Orrie. I can feel him kicking." I can tell I'm not screaming. Somehow, I know I'm not screaming.

"Isn't there anything you can do right now?" he beseeches.

"No, I'm really sorry. It has to be a normal delivery." I hear the verbal quotes around "normal".

Orrie turns his gaze to me as I bob back and forth on the chair. "She's not going to survive until Tuesday."

"What did I do wrong?" Tears pour from my eyes. "Is this because I was late for my ultrasound? You said it was okay if I went away with Orrie and missed the appointment. He's away so much. I thought it would be good to go with him." I look simultaneously at the doctor and Orrie.

"No. You did nothing wrong," the doctor asserts. "These things just happen sometimes. Often it's attributed to lack of folic acid intake."

I sit up straighter, passionately clinging to a thread of hope. "Well, then everything must be okay. It must be a mistake, then. I've been taking folic acid for the past couple of years."

The doctor looks at me, crumpling her face. "There's always a chance there's been a misdiagnosis, but I really wouldn't count on it. These things are pretty apparent and I don't want you to get your hopes up. There's virtually no chance there was a mistake."

"But ... I ... I took folic acid," I stammer.

"It has nothing to do with being late with the ultrasound." Orrie's voice is mechanical and slow. "That's just a mechanism to see how the baby is doing, it doesn't hurt or help the baby." It is obvious Orrie's lawyering instincts are taking over. He's saying this in the doctor's presence so I can hear her medical response. This will protect him from any irrational blame about going away with him on his business trip. It's something I would do if I were still a lawyer. But I'm not. I'm nothing anymore.

The doctor looks at Orrie, then me. "No, it has nothing to do with the ultrasound."

"I know that," I cry.

"Are you sure there's no chance everything is okay?" Orrie asserts.

"Well, there's always a chance, but as I said, I don't want you to get your hopes up. Actually, I strongly caution you against it for your own sake."

I fully collapse into my chair. "So my baby is dead," I moan.

"No, it's not dead, but it isn't capable of surviving outside of the womb. I want you to know you have the option of going full term, but the outcome will be the same. It's usually in the best interest of the mother to be induced."

"My baby isn't an 'it'," I whisper. "You keep saying 'it'. I want that to stop right now. Refer to my baby as he or she."

Orrie looks at me for a second, then upwards as if he's praying. "So she has to go through labor?"

"Yes, I'm sorry."

"Will it feel the same?" I ask.

"I can't really say, because each labor is different for every woman. I think generally it's easier because the baby is smaller."

"I'm going to die. I just want to die. I'm not capable of going through this."

"I have a number for a grief counselor. I think you should call her tonight," the doctor advises.

"What are we going to tell people, Orrie? Everyone knows. We told everyone. I'm six months along. This doesn't happen at six months. Everything is supposed to be okay after three months. Why didn't you know about this before?" I blame the doctor. "You listened to his heartbeat. Why didn't you tell me? You said my baby was healthy," I yell at her.

"There was no way for me to know this. I'm really sorry. Here are the numbers for the counselor and the hospital. You should call both of them tonight. Do you want to wait here for a few minutes to compose yourselves?"

I pull my vacantly staring eyes away from the tile floor and look at her through blurry tears. "Everyone keeps asking us that. Do we look decomposed?"

"The grief counselor is also a nurse, so if you have any questions, she'll be able to answer them," the doctor says as she opens the door.

"I'm going to die, Orrie," I wail once we're alone.

"No, you're not."

"But I want to. I really, really do. I just want to die."

We stay in the exam room for a few silent minutes and then slowly walk back to the car.

My baby is going to die.

Die.

My

baby

is

going

to

die.

I guess every mother has this knowledge to some degree. Without birth, there is no death. We could put an end to dying if we all stopped having children. Someone in

Hollywood should start a movement. They're always aching for something to stand up for.

I remember when I first held Duet in my arms, I actually prayed God would let me die before her. I didn't even thank God for granting me this amazing present. I just wanted to make sure I would never have to know what it's like not to have her. I loved her so much within three seconds of her outward existence I couldn't imagine living without her in my life. Still, I don't think I ever thought about her dying. I never looked at her red, naked body and thought she was going to permanently expire sometime in the future.

Will I be able to hold my baby? How am I going to hold my baby? I won't even get to like this baby and the person who will never develop. I know I'll always love him or her; but I will never be blessed with the wonderful experience of liking my child.

I'll never like my baby.

My baby is going to die.

I keep repeating these phrases over and over in my head like some sort of sick mantra. In an awful way, it's making me feel calmer.

One of the car tires crashes over a huge pothole, breaking me out of my trance. "What are you thinking?" Orrie asks.

"Nothing. Just thinking."

"It's going to be okay, Avril."

"No, it's not. It's never going to be okay again. And if you tell me otherwise, you're just going to make things worse."

CHAPTER 15

I've never felt so lost and alone. I'm sitting here with a full womb and a baby who is going to leave it, never to connect with me again. I feel empty inside, and I don't want to because I don't want the baby to feel unloved or unwanted. This is the only existence he's ever going to have so I want it to be as fulfilling as possible. Living with an undead mother isn't going to make his last days any better. I feel like I'm in stasis because I don't want to really feel yet. It would be too selfish to do so.

I think the baby is a boy. So does Orrie. We don't know why except it feels like everything has been completely opposite to what we went through with Duet's birth, so we figure the sex must be contrasting as well. It only makes sense in this nonsensical sphere.

Before the ultrasound, I was full of joy anytime I felt the baby move. Now when I feel him wiggle, I get elated for a split second, then realize that in a couple of days, I have to deliver him only to see him die. He might die right away, or it might take much longer, no one knows. He might cry when he's born. That's something else we will have to wait to find out. It's horrific enough to know I'm going to have to bury a child. Knowing I'm the only life force he has is beyond devastating. Once the mother/child umbilical bond is broken, he will die. And I have to experience this knowledge every second until I deliver the baby. I'm honestly not sure how I'm going to deal with the delivery. Mostly, it's hard to recognize the most difficult part of all this is yet to come. It will be a normal delivery in the physical sense. I will be induced and have a normal birth. It just won't be a normal outcome.

I start to pray to God to help me, and then I stop because it just feels like a waste of time. I don't necessarily feel angry with God; it's more like I have lost any connection with Him. There's a big, empty void in the heavens. I prayed every night for the baby to be healthy, and he's not. I prayed every night with the same conviction for Duet to be healthy and she is. So why does God answer for one child and not the other? I sense God is listening, just not all of the time. Beforehand, I was even so cocky in my belief that I was praying for God's will each night instead of asking for things. *If you want me to be pregnant, then let me be pregnant. If you want the baby to be a boy, then let him be a boy.* I never thought I was giving God the option to kill my baby. I wouldn't have given Him the choice if I thought this was going to be the result. I was going to ask Orrie if he is mad at God, but I don't know if I want to find out, so I don't think I'll ask.

I don't even feel like I'm having a crisis of faith because I'm still so numb. A crisis sounds so dramatic. I feel nothing except a dull, sharp pain like I'm slowly ripping my neck open with an old, rusty razor. It's like I'm living out my worst fear, and for some reason I am dealing with it. I no longer have a caring God or a viable baby. Pass the carrots, please.

I haven't stopped believing in God, necessarily. I still know He exists, but in the moment I think of Him more as an omniscient being who knows all but does nothing. We pray because we need to. To feel we have absolutely no control over our destinies is too horrible to contemplate. We need to have some input for fate's impacts. Praying fulfills that need, but otherwise it's futile.

Now pass the peas.

After I heard the baby wouldn't survive, I thought maybe this was a test of faith for me. Maybe if I believed enough in God, we would find out this was just a mistake and everything is okay. I wasn't testing God. I just thought maybe God wanted to see how much I believed in him. If faith can move mountains, then surely he can make a technician fallible. But after thinking it over for a while, I realized it wasn't psychologically healthy to think this way. It would be too devastating emotionally to find out yet again that my baby is going to die after having false hope. I think that would certainly break me, and I have to be strong for Duet and Orrie. Plus, it would dishonor my baby's memory if I lost my mind completely.

Two days ago, I would have left a room if someone dared to declare God was uncaring. I would have been too scared to be part of the conversation because I wouldn't want to feel the wrath of God by proximity. Now I feel there's nothing more He can do to me, so I feel liberated in my apathy, even though I'm choking in my betrayal. I haven't been let down by God since I started believing in Him. It was quite easy to believe something when my faith was never truly tested. I don't even know how to cope with disaster. You watch atrocities happen on television or read about it in the paper, but you're always detached from it. You read about a woman whose child died of SIDS and you think how terrible, but that's not my reality. I had a cushion between tragedy and me.

I had a falsely perfect life and now I am real.

I am the real world.

Do you hear me, God? Do you feel anything about what you're doing to me? To the world? Do you care?

It kills me that I don't think He does. If this is the ultimate test of faith, I guess I'm failing quite miserably.

I sense a presence and open my eyes to see that Orrie has come up to the bedroom to check on me. "Do you want some chicken soup?"

"No, thank you, Orrie."

He looks at me for a moment from the doorway. "A tuna and cheese sandwich?"

"Nope. I'm fine, thanks," I mumble as I turn over in my bed to look out the window. It's raining outside and large drops of pooled mist are coming in through the screen, getting the bed wet.

"You'd better close the window. It's starting to get cold in here."

"Yep," I nonchalantly agree, but make no movement.

Orrie waits a couple of minutes and then wiggles in between the bed and the wall to shut the window. He looks outside and quietly comments on how overcast it is today. I politely nod into my pillow. It's amazing I can be so civilized when I'm internally screaming in horror. Is Orrie screaming too? If one were to take off the physical shells and the skin and the organs and get a peek at our souls and mental states, would you just see two blobs of agony writhing around the house saying please and thank you and talking about the weather?

I look back to see if I can sense any torture vibrating from Orrie's inner core, but he's already gone downstairs. I wonder if I should check on him to see how he's doing, but a piece of me doesn't care enough to get out from the covers. I don't care how either of us is doing. It somehow feels safer not to deliberate. The numbness and my bed sheets are the only protection I have at the moment.

I haven't even held Duet today. She came towards me with her arms outstretched this morning but I ran into the bathroom, listening to her cry until Orrie came over to comfort her. *"Everything's okay, sweetie. Mommy just has to go pee. She'll be out in a minute."* I stayed in the bathroom for two hours until I couldn't hear any voices in the house.

I circle the blankets tightly around me and start to cry. I trace my fingers around my stomach. I really love this baby. I don't want him to ever think he was ever a mistake, because he isn't. He's a wonderful baby created by God. I feel very blessed to have been a part of his life for this short time. I can feel him moving all the time. I know he's content and will never experience pain or regret, so that's a great blessing. He is going straight to heaven, which is a gift most of us don't get to enjoy. I guess this begs the question why any of us ever experience life itself if it is so much better to die beforehand.

I have no answer for this. No one does.

I finally fall asleep for a bit. When I wake up, I reach over to open my laptop. The Internet is an amazing resource, it truly is. I can sit here looking up information on anencephaly without having to talk to anyone. I go to a variety of search engines and see what hits come up when I type in the dreaded "A" word. The diversity of the pages is amazing. Some even knew what I meant when I spelled anencephaly wrong. Now that I know how to spell it, the word is forever tattooed in my mind.

A
N
E
N
C
E
P
H
A
L
Y

It almost seems like a pretty word if its definition wasn't so ugly. I look at sites dedicated to children who have died from anencephaly or other disorders. I read the blogs of mothers who have gone through similar experiences. I can do all of this while freely crying and bawling and I don't need to have any regard for my physical composure or mental poise. I feel so disturbingly free.

Orrie has been the official spokesperson for the death parade. He kept his composure long enough to tell all of our family plus a couple of our close friends. I'm the only one who saw him break, and that was entirely by accident. Last night after he put Duet to bed, he ran to the kitchen, turning on the faucets while he howled quietly into the sink. I could hear him from the dining room but I didn't bother going over to comfort him. I couldn't break the hold of gravity to rise from the table. I wanted to, but I just couldn't. I recognize he has been a tower of strength to take care of the family details, but I selfishly just sank into the table and let him shake in the kitchen. I am comfortable with my apathy. It's all I have at the moment.

Orrie talked to the grief counselor last night for about an hour. I listened in, but I wasn't capable of talking to her. Joanie has been calling every hour on the half hour. She has even showed up twice to see if I would talk to her. I know she's freaking out. She's my sister and I love her. I know she desperately wants to help me because I've never been without her in a crisis, but I can't really talk to her yet. There's no use. I will just end up crying, so that will turn into a pretty useless conversation. It's not that I don't want her to see me cry. I don't want to see her hurt. It would make things worse for me. This is something we can't do together. As much as that makes me lonely, it needs to be my journey alone. Orrie told me Joanie offered to take care of all the funeral arrangements, but we're not going to have a funeral. I can't see how looking at a tiny casket would be good or therapeutic for anybody.

My mother has been gracious enough to leave me alone after Orrie told her I really couldn't see anyone. Orrie told my brothers what's happening, but I'm not sure if anyone knows where Dad is so we can let him know he won't be having the grandchild he wasn't aware he was going to have.

I stare at the laptop screen for another couple of hours before stumbling downstairs to instruct Orrie that Duet should stay at Mom's place while we wait to go to the hospital. I would like to visit her before we make the big trek. Aside from that, I am not capable of being with my daughter. I don't really feel like a mother right now. I have a baby in my womb who will die as soon as he leaves it and that's all I can deal with. My maternal instincts are frazzled. Orrie just blankly nods his head and tells me that he has taken some time off work. I don't ask him, but I wonder how a lawyer can do that. Aren't there court dates and issues that have to be dealt with? Aren't there murderers or child molesters who need to be tended to? Maybe someday when I care more, I'll inquire about it. Right now it just doesn't matter.

Nothing matters.

Nothing.

CHAPTER 16

Orrie clutches the steering wheel so tightly his knuckles have turned white. "We're almost at your mother's," he says.

"Is it a good idea to visit Duet before we go? It might make her miss us." I pull my purse to my chest, hugging it like it's a lifeline. "Do you think it might be a bit mean to pop our heads in at Mom's place and then go again? Besides, I don't think I want to see Mom. She might try to talk to me."

"We said we would. I think it would be a good idea," Orrie asserts, closing the conversation. I secretly hate him for being so authoritative. Who is he to tell me what to do? I'm an adult; I can make my own decisions. I can –

"What do you think? We don't have to if you don't want to."

"I think that would be fine," I reply.

Orrie takes a sharp left and I feel the seatbelt tighten across my belly. I'm about to berate him for driving so erratically but then I decide to shut up. What's the point? Maybe we'd be lucky if we got in a tragic car accident before getting to the hospital. It would definitely be easier to deal with.

"You know, it's really weird we don't have a will or anything. You'd think you would be the first person to have all of this done," I bring up out of the blue.

"Why's that?"

"Well, two reasons. First – you're a lawyer. You're probably around wills and stuff every day. Second – you're the most organized person I know. It's completely out of character."

"I'm a walking puzzle," Orrie mutters.

"Why are you trying to joke about this? Are you afraid of death?"

"No."

"I never really thought about death until this week," I announce. "I mean - I rationally knew I was going to die, but it never seemed applicable. Now everything is applicable. There's no foundation anymore. Anything can happen."

Orrie frowns. "There was always the possibility anything could happen. Nothing has changed."

"How can you say that? Everything has changed. Nothing is safe anymore. You could die. I could die. Other things could happen." I don't mention the possibility that something could happen to Duet. I can't even deal with that prospect.

"I don't mean to downplay what you said. I just mean outside of us nothing has changed. We are just more aware of the potential calamity."

"Calamity," I snort.

Orrie looks over. "What?"

"You're the only person I know who would use the word calamity."

"What's that supposed to mean?"

"Nothing. Forget it."

We drive along for another couple of miles. Before we get to Mom's lane he asks again what I meant. I don't have an answer for him, so I just shrug my shoulders and stare out the windshield for a couple of minutes before I open the car door.

"Mommy!" Duet shrieks as she sees me come up the stairs. "Come over here, I want to show you something." She takes me by my hand before I have a chance to get my coat and shoes off. I clumsily wiggle everything off in the entrance and trot along beside her to her blocks and imaginary world.

"See?" She points. "That's where the dragons live."

"Are they good dragons or bad dragons?" I ask, trying my best to be normal.

She looks confused. "Why would bad dragons be there?"

"No reason," I shrug. "I just wanted to be sure. I assumed they were good, but it's always good to ask and be sure."

I look over at Orrie who is getting a huge hug from my mother. I hope she doesn't try to hug me. I haven't even let Orrie touch me since I heard the news. It's like I have a huge raw rash all over my skin and I don't want to rub the pus off on anyone. I nod to my mother in lieu of saying hi. Orrie whispers something in her ear before she comes over to see me.

"How are the roads?" Her eyes are red.

"Good. There aren't any big puddles or anything," I respond. "It's fitting weather for a day like today."

"Yes," she nods. "What's it called in theatre when the weather works with the mood of the play?"

"I don't know. Orrie would know."

"Yeah," she sighs but neither of us asks him.

"Well, we better get going," I say.

"No," Duet yells. "You have to stay. We're all staying here."

I give her a big hug. "No, sweetie. Mommy and Daddy are going away for a little bit and then we'll be back home for good."

She stomps her foot. "But you've already been away."

"No, we've just been home preparing for going away," I explain. "We haven't been away yet."

"Then why wasn't I there?"

"Because your grandmother wanted to have a nice, long visit with you. She loves you and wants to see you more often. We'll all play when we get back. It will just be a couple of days."

"It will be forever," she whines.

"Don't get upset, Du. There's no reason to." I give her another big squeeze. "Mommy loves you. Now go give a goodbye hug to Daddy."

"But I don't want you to go," she continues.

"Neither do I," I slip.

"Well, don't then."

"Sometimes adults have to do things they don't want to. It's a part of being a mommy and being a grown-up."

"I never want to be a grown-up."

"Don't say that," I snap, harshly enough to make Duet's forehead crumple. "Of course you do," I softly explain. "Being an adult is fun. One of my biggest dreams is that you'll be a really fun adult who will play with me when I get older."

"Well, okay then. I'll be an adult. But not for a long, long, long, long time."

I smile. "That sounds great." I look up at Orrie. He has my coat ready to go. We exchange places, put on our boots, Orrie says his goodbyes to Duet, and then we tread back down the stairs and out the door towards adulthood.

CHAPTER 17

"We should have talked more about what we're going to do with the baby," I declare in the middle of the highway.

"What do you mean?" Orrie sharply turns his head towards me. "With the funeral?"

"Yeah, there's that too – we're going to have to explain to everyone we're not having a funeral. But I was thinking more about what we're going to do after the baby is born. I want to hold him. Do you?"

"Yes, of course," Orrie affirms like he never thought otherwise.

"I'm so sorry I haven't been there for you, Orrie."

"It doesn't matter." I think he's going to say more but he stops there.

"There's so much we haven't decided."

"I've taken care of all the funeral arrangements," Orrie sheepishly admits.

"You what?" I shoot at him.

"I would have talked to you about it, but you know..."

"I bought smokes," I declare.

Orrie just stares at the road, not hearing me.

"I bought cigarettes this morning when we got gas. I'm going to have one now."

"What?" Orrie asks, finally looking over at me.

"I'm going to have a cigarette. I'm going to have many cigarettes before we get to the hospital."

"But you don't smoke." Orrie's tone is the one he usually reserves for reasoning with Duet.

"So?"

"What are you talking about? Do you smoke? Have you been smoking?"

"No. But I want to."

"But you don't smoke," Orrie asserts, reasonably.

"At first, I didn't want to hold the baby," I ramble, as if neither of us spoke of anything else. "I didn't want to after what that technician creature from the ultrasound said. She said he didn't have a head, Orrie. How could she be so mean? What was she thinking? The doctor said he will have a head. I can't even believe someone would dehumanize a little baby like that. I did research. I …"

"I had a word with her," Orrie says.

"You what?"

"I went down to the hospital and explained to her supervisor that what she said was completely inappropriate. Her name is Shelley Pickens. It seems to mean a lot when a lawyer makes a formal complaint at the hospital – much more than when a father does. I was told she's been reprimanded and acknowledges what she said was unprofessional. She seems to feel sorry for what she said. Don't worry; we're not suing her or anything. We don't have to deal with it any further. It's over."

"We're not what?" I stare at the side of his head, incredulous. I notice that he has a few grey streaks by his ears that weren't there before. "You did what?" I repeat.

"I didn't think you were up to it. Besides, it was something that had to be taken care of immediately," Orrie explains in his attorney voice. He starts to drive a bit faster with a little less control. "Maybe we should talk about this later. Why did you buy cigarettes?"

"What else have you 'taken care of' this week?" I ask.

"That's it."

"Okay..."

"Why did you buy cigarettes?" Orrie repeats.

"Do we still want to go with Colin if it's a boy, and Angel if it's a girl?" I ask, ignoring the immediate inquiry.

"Yeah, I still think that's fine. How about you?"

"They both sound good to me."

Nothing like a pragmatic conversation in the face of tragedy. It keeps the mind clear. Or fogged. Not sure which.

Don't care.

Orrie looks over at me a couple of times and then returns his gaze to the road. "I was thinking, Avie, maybe it wouldn't be a good idea for you to hold the baby if he or she is deformed."

"Why not? I'm strong enough."

"It's not a question about your strength." He clenches his jaw so I know he's lying. "It's more about how you're going to remember the baby."

"I'll still have fond memories if there's a deformity."

"Have you seen any pictures of babies with anencephaly? Any on the internet?"

"No," I concede. There were some available on the sites I visited, but I could never get myself to click on the photos. "Have you?"

"No, but I don't have the same association with the baby as you do. Right now, he or she is in your belly and maybe you want to keep that memory instead of having a vision of a baby who doesn't look right."

"What do you mean 'look right'? I don't care what the baby looks like. I'm his mother."

"The doctor told me we should be prepared. The baby is going to be much smaller than when Duet was born because he or she is going to be premature. And there might be other things to take into consideration."

"Like what?"

Orrie stares at the road for a bit before answering. He looks over at me and tilts his head to the side. "The baby's eyes might be bigger than normal."

"Would they be open?"

"No, not at this stage."

"What else?"

"I don't know, Avie. I just don't want you to take on something you're not prepared to deal with. This is a forever moment. When did you start smoking?"

"And I think if I didn't see or hold my baby, I would regret it forever. I've actually thought about it for a while, Orrie. At first, I didn't think I would want to because it would be too difficult; but after reading other people's experiences on the Internet, there seems to be a general consensus that it helps with closure if you hold the baby. Otherwise you don't get to say goodbye."

"On the Internet ..." He starts to mutter something but shifts the gear instead, passing the car in front of us.

"What?" I demand, feeling judged.

He ignores the question. "If the baby is alive when he or she is born, the doctor gave us the option of being there until the baby passes away. Either that or a nurse can be with the baby."

"What did you say?"

Orrie's hands tighten on the wheel. "I said I'd think about it."

"Seriously?"

He shifts gears to pass the car ahead of us. "What do you mean?"

"What's to think about?" I ask.

Orrie looks over without breaking his composure, but with a wet face. "It's a very serious question, Avril. It's probably the most serious issue I've ever had to deal with. I wanted to think about it."

"And what do you think?" I ask, softening.

"I want to be there the moment he or she passes away."

"Me too."

"Are you sure?"

"Yes, I don't have to think about it. I just know."

Orrie looks over to see if I'm being venomous; but I'm not. It's just the truth. I just know. I light a cigarette, and Orrie doesn't say a thing.

The rest of the drive is silent. We don't even have music playing. I get lost in the rhythmic sound of the wipers going back and forth on the windshield. I scrunch over in my seat so that my cheek rests on the cold window. It leaves an oily stain on the glass that I wipe clean with my sleeve as we arrive at the hospital. We get out of the vehicle in the dank, gassy underground parking garage with its sprinklings of pigeon poop in all of the corners. I hang around the car door for a bit after it's shut because I don't want to move. I don't want to go through the swinging doors and up the elevator. I don't want to start this process because I don't think I'm ready.

I'm never going to be ready.

"Avie?" Orrie calls from the other side of the car.

"Yeah?"

"Are you coming?"

"Yeah."

I move one foot in front of the other. This is what we've been preparing for. This is what all of the tears and trials have been about. I subconsciously pat my stomach and Orrie catches me. "It will be okay, Avril. We've come this far." I nod, keeping one foot going in front of the other.

"There isn't any cooing," I say.

"What?"

"There's mess everywhere from the pigeons, but none of them are around to coo."

Orrie presses the up button to call the elevator. "Maybe they're outside flying around."

"I wonder if they'll poop all over the car."

"We can clean it off when we get home."

"True. It's not a big deal, I was just speculating." The elevator arrives and we step on.

Orrie pushes the button for the fifth floor. "We can go to one of those automatic car washes on the way home."

"That sounds like a good idea."

The elevator dings as we reach the admitting floor. When Orrie was making the arrangements from home, the nurse on the phone told us everything would be taken care of. The people at admitting would know what was going on. *"You shouldn't have to explain everything. There should be a note."*

There is no note.

"First name?" The woman at the admitting desk asks.

"Avril Bale."

"Is Avril your first name?"

"Yes, sorry. Avril. Just Avril. My middle name is Echo. My father was really into the ancient myths. He really liked the name Echo but didn't want that to be my first name because he didn't want me to be someone who didn't think for herself." I lean my elbows on the counter. "Apparently, if it was my second name, it wouldn't matter so much. My father named me after a French nurse named Avril. He said she was a really kind woman. I'm the only one he named. My mother named my sister and brothers after family members."

"Last name Bale? B-a-l-e?" The nurse obviously doesn't find my family's naming history of any consequence.

"Yes."

"Is this your first time in for a delivery?"

"No, I was here a couple of years ago when I had my first baby."

"So, this is your second?"

"Yes." I'm not sure what I'm answering. My hands start to shake.

"Do you have insurance?"

"Yes."

"Can I see your card?"

I give her all of my information, including my driver's license and a customer card from a coffee chain. I know she doesn't have any need for it, but I want this process to be over. I figure too much information is better than too little. Anything to shut her up and leave me alone. Then I realize I'm patting my belly. I look around and it's like an orchestra of musical fingers. All of the women sitting in the waiting room are patting their bellies while they're waiting or being served. I realize this is the unit where all expectant mothers dwell, regardless of the impending consequences. I wonder how many of their pregnancies are going well. I study their faces for any signs of tragedy, but each of them just looks bored. I wonder if I look bored or sad. I know I have more wrinkles than I did two weeks ago, and my eyes look hollow no matter how much makeup I use to cover up the shadows. Are people looking at me, wondering if something is wrong? Am I upsetting the other ladies?

"Your health plan covers a dual room, so you'll be sharing with someone else."

"No, that's not possible. I can't share with anyone. Would she have a baby?"

"Yes, of course. You'll be in the maternity ward."

"No, I can't do that." My voice rises. I can feel panic rising with it. Orrie senses something is amiss and swiftly comes to my side.

"What's up?" he asks.

"They're going to make me share a room with a baby."

"No, we were told we'd have a private room. If that's not possible, we'll just pay extra for one." He leans in closer. "It is special circumstances," he whispers.

The administrator's face softens. She doesn't ask what sort of circumstances but Orrie fills her in anyway. I look around to see if anyone is listening. I don't want anyone to know. I want to be part of this pregnant room, patting our healthy fetuses through our healthy bellies. I don't want to be the odd woman out.

"Sorry – I have your papers right here. You're on the seventh floor. You'll be in a private room."

I zone out, letting Orrie take care of the details. I don't even think I have bones left. My body slumps, allowing whatever cartilage is left to keep me from melting into the floor. Maybe I'll just die and all of this will be over with. Maybe a runaway bed will hit me, bashing my head open against a sterilized metal tray. Maybe a miracle will happen and everything will be okay.

Anything but this.

I can't take this.

I just can't.

I get to my room and I'm immediately met with a nurse who points to the clothes I need to put on before getting into my bed. Orrie sits on a chair while I get changed in the bathroom. I come back and get under the sheets just before another nurse knocks on the door, asking if it is okay to come in.

The nurse peeks her head through the door before entering. "Are you comfortable?"

"I don't care."

"Excuse me?" The nurse asks, kindly.

"Yes, I'm fine. I'm fine, fine, fine. I'm fine."

"Avril..." Orrie starts.

"I'm great," I spit out, immediately feeling guilty for my nastiness. "I'm sorry," I say to the nurse. "I'm not in a good frame of mind."

"I know, dear," the nurse comforts while rubbing my back. I usually can't stand it when people call me dear, but she somehow empowers the word in the way she says it. It's like she means it, or something.

"Right now, we want to go over the procedure with you. Plus, we need to get a conclusive ultrasound. We also want you to talk to the grief counselor later on today."

I start crying and Orrie comes over to hold me. "Am I allowed to stay with her?"

"That's it, dear. Get it out," the nurse soothes. She puts her hand on Orrie's shoulder. "Yes, you can stay with her the entire time."

Later that afternoon, the doctor sits on the edge of my bed, showing me the pill that will induce me. I have no idea why she's showing me what it looks like. It's not like I don't believe her, or anything. I have no illusions she's just going to pretend to induce me with a placebo. The doctor explains how long this should take and what I should expect and I should buzz the nurse any time I feel uncomfortable. "Things could start rolling in a couple of hours; but there's no way of knowing for sure. Each birth is different."

Rolling.

"Rolling along" has always had a positive connotation before. Now "rolling" doesn't sound like so much fun. I keep looking at the doctor while she's speaking to me, but I have absolutely no idea what she's saying. I'm losing my ability to pay attention. Have I ever truly listened to people? Do people ever listen to me? Is anyone capable of ever really hearing what someone says, or do they just listen to the words, making their own interpretation of what was said? I feel Orrie pat my leg, or maybe it's the doctor. Maybe there's a poisonous spider in my bed that just walked over my thigh. Who knows? Who cares. I had another ultrasound earlier today to confirm the baby has anencephaly. It was confirmed and here I sit. No turning back now. No hope left, no luck left, no feelings left. While we were at the ultrasound, the doctor asked me if I wanted to know if it's a boy or a girl. I looked at Orrie to see what he thought. He told the doctor we might as well know, and are told we're going to have a boy tomorrow.

We are going to have a Colin.

CHAPTER 18

I'm now entering hour twenty of the labor process. The baby still wants to be with me. I tell Orrie I'm afraid the baby doesn't want to leave me because he knows what's happening and doesn't want to face it. He wants to be with his mother and feel the warmth of his only reality. This is his only chance at an existence. When he comes into the real world, he will be entering his death. Orrie tells me everything will be all right. Everything will be okay.

Don't worry.

Don't stress.

I feel like bearing down and tell the nurse. "Something new is happening, I think I should go to the birthing chair."

"Do you feel like pushing?" she asks.

"Yes. Something is happening for sure. Can you help me over there?"

The nurse and Orrie maneuver me and my morphine drip over to the bathroom where they help me sit down. I get to have morphine because the negative consequences to the baby are inconsequential. I feel a big gush and my water breaks all over the birthing bucket, splashing up into the small of my back. I think I even hear some of it splatter onto the floor. I aimlessly look around at the liquid goo pooling around my feet.

Orrie is shell-shocked by the spectacle on the floor. He looks up at me and regains his composure. "Get her into the room," Orrie gently directs, "so she can be close to the bed after the baby arrives."

The nurse agrees this is a good idea, so the chair, the morphine and I get ready to be wheeled back to the room. I feel another contraction and tell them to stay put. The nurse moves around beside me, cleaning up my water. I feel yet another contraction and something swooshes out of my body.

"I think I just had him." I feel like I'm choking on my own spit. I try to move but it really hurts.

The nurse comes over immediately, telling me it's the baby. She moves me into position so they can cut the cord.

The cord.

The life force.

The beginning of the end for my little boy.

I am still sitting with my hands between my knees when the nurse comes back and asks me if I want to see my son. "He's alive and he's moving," she announces. "He's with your husband right now. We're just wrapping him up in a blanket."

"Does my husband want me to see him?" I ask.

"I'm not sure I understand," she replies, softly.

"Does Orrie want me to see him? Can you ask him if he wants me to?"

"Certainly. Do you want some help up on the bed first?"

"Okay. I thought I should wait here for the placenta." That's me. Nothing like being practical in the middle of a life-altering tragedy.

"There's no need, dear. Let's get you up on the bed. Your body can take care of that there. You'll be more comfortable. You've been through a lot. Best to be comfy."

I can't believe Colin is alive. I feel so proud he is such a fighter. My little soldier. My baby.

Orrie comes in with Colin. He is so incredibly tiny. He doesn't even fully reach from my hand to my elbow. Orrie is crying and doesn't bother to hide it.

"Can I see him?" I ask. "Should I?"

"Yes," Orrie chokes. He sits down on the bed beside mine and I look down at our son. He looks perfect. He looks breakable. I don't want to hurt him because I'm still pretty shaky. I tell Orrie to keep holding him for a little bit longer until I get my bearings. "I'll just look at him for a while."

Orrie and I talk to each other and to Colin until I'm ready. When Duet was born, I couldn't believe how much she looked like Orrie. When she first lay with me after the delivery, it was like a miniature version of my husband was curled in the crook of my arm.

"He has your chest," I tell Orrie.

"Don't," he mumbles. "I'm not ready to hear that yet."

"Sorry."

"That's okay."

"Can I hold him now?"

"Sure." Orrie carefully places him in my arms. I look down at my baby and touch his little hands and his tiny feet. His eyes are closed like they're glued shut. His little lips are puckered out like he still thinks he's drinking the amniotic fluid. He doesn't seem to be breathing.

"Do you think he's still alive?" I whisper to Orrie.

"Yes, I think so."

I try not to think about how incredibly strange it is that I don't know whether my baby is alive or has passed away in my arms. He is so still. I don't feel any connection in that sense. I look down at him in love and adoration; but I can't figure out for the life of me if he is still alive.

The nurse then comes in to check on me so I hand Colin back to Orrie. I lean back and she checks to see if I'm bleeding. Apparently I am. A lot. Much more than I should be. After that, they proceed to check on me quite frequently and then a doctor comes in for a peek. I guess I'm gushing out a lot more blood than they're comfortable with. I really don't care at this point. Orrie and Colin are asked to leave the room while I am assessed. After a short while, I'm being whisked away to the O.R. for surgery. Orrie comes back to see me off, and the look on his face is enough to break my heart. Actually the entire picture would be gut-wrenching if I were with it enough to feel interest. I'm aware enough from the conversation with my doctor to know my husband is holding my dying baby in his arms, standing beside the bed of his wife as she is wheeled away, maybe never to come back again. I take another look back at them and Orrie is holding Colin's cheek next to his, shielding himself against the whole ordeal. I begin to lift my hand to wave goodbye, but then think better of it and just limply lay there as they take me away.

I look at everything as I pass through the hallway. I try to count the ceiling tiles, but they are whizzing by too quickly for me to keep a running tally. It feels really strange to think of things like this before dying.

Am I dying?

Am I concerned? I can't for the life of me be bothered with hanging on. I try to conjure up an image of Duet to take with me into the operating room, but even this doesn't affect me. I honestly don't care if I die or not. It's a really weird sensation and I'm dulled enough to actually think about it analytically instead of emotionally. Is this what it's like when old people die? I'm not even remotely scared.

I'm not old, though.

I should care.

Is this on par with being suicidal? I think about this as I wheel by another hallway and I decide it isn't. I didn't make myself hemorrhage. It's not like I stuck a knife between my legs, making the life force bleed out of me. I'm just too tired to fight what might be the inevitable. And this might be my chance to be with Colin. He's with Orrie now, maybe in a few minutes he'll be with me. Will he be a little baby when I meet him? Will I eternally get to be a baby's mother? Would that be a good thing? One of the beauties of parenthood is seeing your child develop – would I be fulfilled in death if Colin were my baby forever?

We wheel by more beds in the corridor and I think of death as the ultimate balancer. It is the one moment everyone experiences equally, no matter how death comes to you, no matter what your life was or what your ultimate after-life experience will be. Conception, birth, life and after-death are all unequal playing fields – one is destined at each of those timelines to be better, stronger, happier, privileged, genetically challenged, poorer, or forever damned. But in that one concrete second death comes, each and every one of us who has ever existed – or will exist – is connected and on par with each other.

We're in the elevator and I look up at the faces of the people who are wheeling me around. What do they think when they take someone to the operating room? Do they internally place bets on who they'll wheel back? Do they care if I live or die? And why should they care if I don't?

I finally get to the operating room, and it's really cold. I hate being cold. I can't believe I'm so bothered by it, but it's really affecting me more than anything else right now.

Colin is dying.

I stick that into my heart just to feel the pain.

I want to hurt.

The doctor or the nurse or somebody who works here (the janitor?) asks me a few health questions. I answer without even thinking. Usually I really try to honestly answer queries such as these. I usually want to ensure I'm 100% correct in my answers when I'm talking to doctors or anyone in authority. I take a moment to wonder why this is so, and I guess I gap out while the interrogator is questioning me.

She bends down closer to look at me. "Avril?"

"Yes?"

"How are you doing?"

"Are you really asking me that?"

"Pardon me?"

"How do you think I'm doing?" I start crying.

"I know, dear. I'm sorry. Are you in any pain?"

"Yes, of course."

"Where then? Where do you hurt?"

I tell her I'm fine and I don't hurt anywhere and everything is okay and don't worry and is Colin dead?

"We don't know, honey," someone in scrubs tells me.

"I had a cigarette on the way here," I declare.

I think they judged me on this, but I'm not entirely sure. I answer a few more questions then get injected with more needles. I am asked to breathe into an apparatus that is placed over my mouth. No chance for screaming now. I don't bother looking for the light at the end of the tunnel. I'm engulfed with black and I think I even chuckle with the appropriateness of it all.

CHAPTER 19

My eye is itchy.

My eye is itchy and I'm really thirsty.

My eye is itchy, I'm really thirsty and I feel like I should get up. But for some reason I can't remember, I don't want to wake up yet. I hear Orrie moving over to the bed and he takes my hand.

"Avie?"

"Yeah?" I say, remembering everything in a flash.

"Are you awake? How are you doing?"

"Is Colin alive?"

"No, he passed away a couple of hours ago."

"Oh."

"Are you all right?"

I'm really tired of that question. I really, really am. I open my eyes and look over at his swollen face. I decide not to be bitter or berate him for inane inquiries. "Yeah, I'm okay. You?"

"I'm okay. I was worried about you."

"Did you know when he died?"

"Maybe we shouldn't talk about that now." I wonder if he's thinking of him or me. I decide not to push it.

"May you live in interesting times," I blurt out.

"What, Avie?"

"I'm just thinking of a Chinese curse. You'd think it's a blessing; but when you say it over and over again, you realize that interesting times aren't usually pleasant."

"Do you feel cursed?"

"Yeah, I do."

"You have a good life overall," he asserts.

"Let's not talk about that now."

I stay in the hospital for two days after Colin's delivery until it's assessed that I'm healthy enough to make the trek home. Orrie stayed with me in a hospital bed beside mine, which was about a foot too short for him, so I know he is definitely ready to leave. I'm warned by the doctors to hold off for a bit with carrying Duet or doing any vacuuming.

Orrie and I don't talk to each other the entire drive home. There doesn't really seem to be any point. What is there to say? What can we resolve? We pick up Duet at my mother's. I wait in the car, pretending I'm asleep. I keep my eyes closed as I hear Duet and Orrie's voices getting louder. Duet's singing "Jingle Bells" and telling Orrie what she wrote to Santa while we were away.

I totally forgot Christmas is coming up next month.

Merry Christmas. God bless us, every one.

CHAPTER 20

Once there were butterflies
Shiny and blue.
Once there were tulips
Glistening anew.
Once there were trees
That grew and grew.
But then someone lit a match and didn't extinguish it properly
and the whole
forest burned down.

The true end.

CHAPTER 21

Funerals are supposed to be held on rainy days when everyone has an umbrella and everybody's clothes are soaked with the torrents of rain and depression. It is quite nice on the day we have Colin's service. I even think birds are chirping. I would say life is deliciously ironic if I didn't have to constantly spit out the acid taste on my tongue.

We weren't supposed to have a funeral. I thought we had decided that, but when the process was in place I apparently was too whacked to give my opinion on the subject. Did everyone else have different memories of my decision?

Our pastor gives a few words. Nobody sings or reads any passages. Colin doesn't even attend. His ashes are still in the crematorium by the hospital. They weren't able to get here in time. Ah, the irony. Premature birth yet late for his own funeral. Acid, acid, acid.

We didn't invite anyone except family. Both of Orrie's parents died years ago so he is used to death. He was an only child, which means we're the only family he has left. There were no friends at the ceremony. I think some were a bit dismayed they couldn't share in the sadness, but this is the way we wanted it, so this is the way it shall be. Only Joanie and Mom were able to attend from my immediate family. The twins sent a really beautiful bouquet of flowers that ended up being bigger than the casket.

Ashes to ashes.

Dust to dust. Little, tiny spoonfuls of unknown dust.

We head to the basement of the church to have some sweets and egg salad sandwiches. I usually throw up when I eat or even smell an egg sandwich, but today I deliberately make a beeline to a plate full of them, taking a couple. I force the pieces to slowly slide down my throat.

"Where's Duet?" the pastor asks.

"She's with a sitter for the day. She still doesn't know," I say between mouthfuls.

"Ah."

"She's so young," I continue to explain. "She doesn't need to know. We're not lying to her. We're just not telling her."

The pastor nods again so I ramble on. "She stayed with my mom while we were at the hospital. She didn't know what was going on then, either."

The pastor looks at me and asks if I would like for him to pop by for a visit sometime. I tell him we'd prefer to keep to ourselves for a bit. "But we're doing really well, though. Perfect really. I can't believe how well we're dealing with this. With Colin. With Colin dying."

The pastor nods as I scoff down another egg sandwich with my tea. "There's no need for Duet to know," I repeat.

The pastor nods again.

"We're going to bury Colin's ashes out front of our house this spring. I guess you're opposed to that, huh?" I ask, trying to get him angry. Anything to get him to stop nodding.

"Opposed to what, Avril?"

"Him not being buried in a cemetery. That's probably something you don't see as proper."

"No, Avril. I think that's a lovely place for your baby to rest. You'll always have him near you."

"Yes, he'll always be near us, it's a lovely place." I'm disappointed he is being so understanding and kind. I look over at the half-eaten plate of egg salad sandwiches, grabbing another one. "So how often do you have funeral services for babies?"

"Not very often." He's not nodding anymore.

"I better go get Orrison. I should see how he's doing."

The Pastor goes back to nodding again. "Yes, dear."

"We're doing fine but it's good to be together."

"Yes, yes." Nod, nod. I shake his hand goodbye, even though we'll be together in the same room eating sandwiches for at least another twenty minutes.

"Take care, Avril. I'll be here."

"Yep," I nod. "Me too. I'll be around."

CHAPTER 22

I'm awake again.
I want to go to sleep but I can't.
I cannot.
I am not permitted.
It's insane.
I should sleep because that's what is good for me and my body, but me and my body won't let me go to sleep.
I'm going to go insane.

Today is my birthday. The date of my birth. I've been around for 32 years and my son was alive for a mere three hours. I've always hated being born so close to Christmas, even as an adult. It always seemed like something special was taken away from me. And now something truly special was taken away from me, so I really don't care anymore about the stolen birthday.

It's insane. I'm going to go insane. What did you get for your birthday, Avril?

I really think I'm losing it. I'm trying to be all healthy and strong, but something inside of me isn't allowing me to keep my strength. Do I have a phantom baby in my womb? Am I haunted? Colin wouldn't haunt me, would he? Is he angry with me? Did I not love him enough? Does he blame me? He wouldn't have the intellectual capacity to know what happened, so does he think I planned all of this? That I didn't want him? I wake up from fake slumber, feeling weak from exhaustion, yet I can't get it together enough to make it to dreamland.

I just want to go to sleep. I'm so tired. Everything would be okay if I could just get to sleep. Can dreamless sleep be my birthday wish, God?

Oh wait – God's not here, he's with Colin.

I used to love sleep. I think I would still be enamored with the sensation if I could get back into the habit. I think about how over my birthday dinner I was telling everyone about how blessed I am, even throughout all these interesting times. And I *am* blessed – so why do I also feel like such a loser? Why do I feel like such a failure in life? And how can I feel like such a failure when I am so blessed? I have a daughter who is so incredibly amazing, and a husband who I love completely. What more can I ask for? But then I keep thinking about losing them through some freak tragedy. I've been having horrific, terrible visions about Duet. The other day, I imagined her little body unmoving on the floor because the ceiling fan fell out of its hinges and crashed down, bashing in her little skull. I actually saw it. I have visions of Duet going under her bed for a lost teddy and her head getting squashed because the bed inexplicibly falls apart from its frame. Then other times when she's a little late coming home with Orrie from wherever they have been, I actually hear Orrie tell me there was a car accident and there was nothing they could do, and I really don't want to see her lifeless body.

And then I see it.

I honestly see it.

I've prayed for the visions to end. I know they aren't a forerunner to anything happening. I know I don't have any powers of foresight. I also know these visions are driving me insane. I can't take it. I don't want to see it. I want to mentally go blind so I don't have to endure thoughts like this. I'd prefer to live in a catatonic state of nothingness than to see these images. Is this normal? Am I seeing things because I know there's a possibility of these sights? That the worst can happen? Or am I seeing these things because I am unbalanced and in need of professional help? Should I seek counseling? There's something in me that just doesn't believe in it. It's like you slip into that couch for life, like the nickels and misplaced socks that get tucked into the crevices. No one ever gets cured – people seem to enter the professional relationship and stay with it longer than any of their personal ones last. Now I'm envisioning myself on the couch, having a heart attack. Well, good. At least it's me dying this time.

I can't look into a future filled with potential loss. I can't live my life in fear of something devastating happening. But then I keep going back to the fact that a catastrophe did happen. What's to stop it from happening again? Stats? Do I have to rely on statistics for my sanity? And are stats in my favor in the first place? Is it statistically possible for every person I love to die by unforeseen and agonizing circumstances? I've proven I defy stats. The occurrence of anencephaly is pretty much impossible. Stats aren't my friend. The possible and the improbable have always existed side by side, but I'm afraid they've become one combined entity so now my entire existence is in danger.

I just want to sleep and wake up. I want to wake up pregnant again with a healthy fetus in my belly who will grow into a beautiful, healthy boy.

Can this be my birthday wish, God? Hello?

But this isn't going to happen. I already gave birth, and my baby died. I literally signed his death certificate right after I signed his birth certificate. I consciously remember doing this. With as much dignity as possible, I took the pen and signed both documents in a row. I wasn't going to cry again. My baby's birthday is the day of his death.

My baby will never realize how it feels for me to hold him. He was too young to recognize or remember that physical sensation. I will always remember holding Colin, but I'll never know how it feels for him to hold me. I just want to feel his little arms around my neck and I want to hear his little squeaky voice call me mommy. I feel like Colin's mother, but I'll never know what it's like to mother him.

Am I being selfish, having all this pain? Feeling this way isn't good for Duet. It's not good for me, either. Or is it? Did I not grieve enough? Was I not sad enough? Am I going to break? I will if I don't sleep soon, but I can't. Why can't I sleep? The aching is unbearable at nights. That's when the howling begins. I try to hold my pillow and pretend it's Colin but it doesn't help. Pillows don't breathe. But then again, neither does Colin.

Why is my body rejecting me? Why can't my mind just stop and leave me in peace? Then I start to think about what's going to happen when my mind actually does stop. Forever. I was always aware I was going to die, but I never actually realized my mortality. People actually die. It's a fact. What if

Duet or Joanie dies before me? What if Orrie dies? Can I take it? What's going to stop it from happening? What's it going to feel like when I take my last breath? It was okay when I went in for surgery because I was so exhausted I didn't care about dying. So is that it? Am I subconsciously trying to get so exhausted I won't care if I die? Do I want to die? I think there's a huge part of me that's afraid to live. To keep living. To keep going with the threat of recurring tragedy. To keep alive through all of the struggles and strife that accompany daily life. Unfortunately, there's no great balancing act that ensures once I reach my capacity of trials, good will come my way. The bad can keep on coming and coming and there's nothing I can do to stop it.

Nothing except get off the train.

And I don't want the train to stop at this juncture - not simply because I'm afraid of death. I desperately want to enjoy life again. But I'm so deathly afraid the good will completely dissolve and I'll be left with a caboose that's as empty as my womb is now. I think about my womb. Is it healthy? Can I have another baby someday? Can I go through the possibility of loss happening again? Would that finally break me, to lose another child?

Would I survive another signature?

I think about Colin's cremated body. I think about the fact there's probably not much dust in the urn. I think about the urn now gathering dust in the funeral home waiting to be transported to where we're going to bury him. Bury his dust. Bury his dust in the dust next spring. I think about the spot where we're going to bury him in our front yard. I've been researching different types of trees that we could plant there in his memory. Will he be peaceful there? Will he be aware on some level that he's there? Will he know we love him? Will he be sad we're not with him all the time? Will he be lonely? Is he lonely in the funeral parlor, sitting amongst all that death?

Can I wish for my birthday that I will be sane?

God? It's 4 am on my birthday.

Hello?

I finally fall asleep, only to ultimately wake up screaming and sobbing. Orrie bolts up, holding me until I stop shaking. He asks me what my dream was about but I tell him I don't remember. He lies back down, pulling me alongside so we spoon, almost desperately.

I know there are theories floating around that a person who dies in her dream can potentially die in real life. Something about the heart stopping. Can a person die from dreaming about another's death? When one is sleeping and not consciously aware of the body's processes, can a person go to sleep and die from crying? Can a body completely dehydrate from loss of tears on a pillow? Sounds like such a tragic way to go. Almost beautiful, in a morbid way.

I just had a dream they were doing the autopsy on Colin. They were cutting up his tiny, tiny body and the operating table was part of a doll's set. The doctors had really small hands because otherwise they couldn't perform the procedure. Aside from those two quirks, it was very non-dreamlike. It was like watching a procedure on a learning channel or something. There was no music or even color to the dream. It was just the mechanical movement of a surgeon's hand cutting open the dead body of my little boy.

I want to take a shower. I feel dirty for having this dream. How can I have such visions? I keep remembering his little face with his little cap covering up his skull. He was so beautiful and so peaceful. I have no idea how I could have destroyed his image with this dream. Now whenever I think of him, the images in my memory will be spliced with this nightmare. I'm such a failure. I couldn't create a healthy baby and now I can't even conceive a healthy image of my child.

I deserve everything that comes to me.

CHAPTER 23

"I think you need help."

My hackles rise. "What's that supposed to mean?" I'm ready to verbally punch back at any accusation that belittles my strength and ability.

Orrie casually continues to dry breakfast dishes from the rack, passing them to me to be put in the cupboard. "I think we should get a cleaning lady to come in once or twice a week to help you with housework."

My eyes narrow. "I'm more than capable of cleaning our house, thank you very much."

"No you're not, Avril. You're still sore, and to be perfectly honest, things have gone downhill around here lately. I'm not passing judgment. I'm not implying you're not trying. I'm not even saying it's important, but I do think we should hire someone to help you out a bit."

"I'm not going to be one of those people who needs a maid. I don't need that hassle."

Orrie drops his towel on the table. "What is that supposed to mean?"

"I get enough ribbing already from everyone about staying home full time, even before all of this happened. I'm supposed to be a lawyer, as well as a parent. I don't need people to think I'm so incapable that I can't make my own bed when I'm home twenty-four hours a day."

"You just had a traumatic experience and are recovering from surgery. I don't think people are in the mood to pass judgment. Besides, who cares what they think? And who are 'they' exactly? Strangers, friends, who?"

"Joanie thinks I should be working. Joanie's friends all think so, too. Most women look at me and pass judgment. It's the way things are."

"You've never mentioned it before."

"It's never bothered me before."

Orrie shakes his head, confused. "So do you want to go back to work?"

"No, I want to stay home and look after Duet," I say.

"Well, do you want some help with that? Just for a little while? I would help out, but I don't have the time. I took too much time off work already."

"Do you think I'm inept, Orrie?"

"No, of course not. I think you need a bit of help for a month or so until things start to sort out and you're back to your old self."

I play around with the bubbles in the sink. "I don't know who my old self is anymore."

Orrie turns to me. I can tell by his face he's debating whether or not he should leave the house ever again. "I'm only kidding," I stress. "Fine. I'll put an ad in the paper today and start interviewing next Monday. Does that sound alright?"

"Only if you're okay with it," Orrie says. "I don't want to pressure you. Maybe we can wait until after Christmas or New Year's. You probably wouldn't get a lot of responses over the holidays. Maybe this can be a Christmas present for the house."

"Wow, the house is really moving up in the family. It never warranted a present before."

"Well, it is the season and all that rot," Orrie smiles.

"I guess I'm a pretty lucky woman if one of the big pressures in my life is to have help around the house," I banter. For a second, it feels like old times.

"I don't want you to read anything into this that isn't there," Orrie reassures. "I just think you should have some help for a bit. I've noticed you haven't been sleeping well lately. This will give you a chance to sleep in a couple of days a week. You're looking really pale lately."

"Are you worried about me?"

"No, of course not." Orrie clenches his jaw, a telltale sign he's lying.

"Well, you'd better get to work so you can make enough money for the staff."

"Do you want to pick up some Christmas gifts after I get home? I shouldn't be too late tonight."

"No. Joanie, Duet and I are going shopping in an hour or so. I'll pick up most of them today."

"Okay. When do you want to pick up Duet's presents?"

"We could do that this weekend, if you're not busy. We're kind of leaving it until the last minute this year."

"Yes, well. That's okay." Orrie knows there's no need to express why that is. No need at all.

After I get back from shopping, I put Duet down for her nap and tackle the help wanted ad. I know that if I don't get started, Orrie will be on my case and I don't want any more tension, especially over something that is intended as a gift. My first draft reads:

Wanted: Someone to come in for a couple of hours twice a week to help out with cleaning and childcare. Mornings preferred.

Hmmm ... let's expand on that:

Wanted: Someone to come in for a couple of hours a week to help out lazy mother who doesn't feel like doing much lately. Mornings preferred so sleeping in is possible.

Nope, not quite. How about:

Wanted: Qualified magician who is experienced in time travel and can teleport mother back in time so she doesn't have to lose her baby. Mornings preferred so this can be accomplished as soon as possible.

Ultimately, I go with something generic. A couple of days later, I have three women who are waiting in my living room sipping decaffeinated coffee because I forgot to get some of the real brew for the interviews. None of them seems anxious or excited about meeting me. I'm positive I'm more nervous than any of them.

I've always hated interviews, especially if I'm the one being interviewed. I have friends who go into interviews with the attitude that they're the ones conducting the dialogue. It is they who decide if they want the job or not. I'm not so bold or fortuitous. I'm the one who brings breath mints because I usually throw up ten minutes before I talk to anyone. I brought gum once and later worried I looked like a cow chewing its cud throughout the entire process. At least I was smart enough to never do that again. I'd rather have puke-breath than look like something that stands on all fours to urinate.

So – are these women interviewing me? Are they the ones who get to decide if they stay in my home? I peek in again through the slats in the swinging doors to see how they're doing. I don't want to go in there, looking like a bored housewife who wants a maid because all her friends have one. At least they won't think I'm rich. One look at our house and they would all know we're middle class at best. Maybe they're all wondering why someone in this income bracket would want to waste their hard earned money on help.

I was going to take Duet to Mom's while I talk to the women, but I decide it will be better if she is running around so I can gauge how they react. It ends up Duet is in a bit of a mood today, which will actually work out well. If one of these women can love Duet through a temper tantrum then she's an ace in my book.

The first person I speak with takes one look at Duet and falls in love with her. I almost don't want to bother with the rest of the interviews because she seems like a perfect fit. Gloria is fifty-two with two adult sons and a daughter. She ended up graduating from university between diapers and drool. She currently works afternoons and evenings at a library in town. She's available two mornings every week before she goes to the library, and she is fine with the fact that it isn't going to be a permanent gig. "I don't have any professional experience with cleaning homes; but with a husband and three kids, I know a lot about it," she laughs.

"I can only imagine," I smile. I want to say something engaging but this is all I can come up with. I'm hoping she's not interviewing me for my communication skills.

She looks at Duet. "Are you going to have more children?"

"Yes, someday." I don't feel like going into detail.

"Are you going to be away in the mornings?"

"No, I'll be here. I have a medical condition, so I need a bit of help for a while." I'm not sure if I am lying to her, but I don't really care. It feels more polished than admitting I don't care anymore if my house is filthy.

We talk for a few more minutes and I shake her hand as she rises from the couch to leave. I tell her I'll let her know by this evening either way. She politely thanks me as she walks down the hallway. I'm confident I'll be seeing her walking through my door again. I end up talking to the other women because I feel I should, but none of them live up to the shine of Gloria.

Orrie will be pleased I'm starting to move on with my life.

The next day I go to mom's place. I'm embarrassed to tell her we're getting a house cleaner, so I keep that piece of info to myself. I know she'll find out at some point. When she does, I'll pretend I thought I told her already.

"So when are you going to put the death notice in the paper?" My mother asks, blowing into her teacup.

I scoop my tea bag from the cup with a spoon and place it on a plate. "Orrie and I decided not to."

Mom's jaw drops. "Why on earth not, dear?"

"We talked about it and we both decided it's something we'd prefer not to do."

"But he was a little person. He deserves a notice."

I frantically stir my tea. "It's not about deserving one. Of course he deserves one. That's not even in question," I ramble.

"Then why not?"

"Because we don't want everyone in the world to feel sorry for us," I tell her.

"Of course people feel bad for you. It's a tragedy. Everyone will feel sorry; you can't help that. Don't be so selfish."

"I feel like everyone is looking and pointing at me as it is."

Mom waves her hand in the air, dismissing me. "Everyone isn't pointing at you. Most people don't even know about it."

"Exactly."

"What? Exactly what?"

"Well, if I were to put a death notice in the local paper, then everyone here would know. I wouldn't just be imagining everyone is talking about me when I go to the bank or the corner store. Everyone would be. 'That's the girl who lost her baby. Something was wrong with his brain or something. Poor thing.' I couldn't take it."

"But what about the people who knew you were pregnant and come up to ask how your baby is coming along? What about people who come up to me? Someone asked your sister about it yesterday and she had no idea what to say. Personally, I have no idea how I'd react. I think I would break down. I'm terrified of that happening. I wouldn't even wish that on your father, and you know how I feel about him."

"I just don't want the world to know. I don't want someone I went to school with fifteen years ago - who barely even remembers my name - to know about this. I don't want my face to be conjured up in some stranger's memory and be associated with this. It's too personal. It's too real. It's too connected to me to belong to someone else. I don't want to be reduced to gossip."

"People just want to know about what's going on in their community," Mom explains.

"And what about the people who have no clue what they're talking about? What if some idiot passes judgment because I didn't carry the baby to full term?"

"No one is that cruel."

"Don't be so naive, Mom. There's a lot of stupidity floating around the collective consciousness."

"I just can't see that happening."

"Well, it has. There are instances of it in the grief book they gave me at the hospital about what other mothers have gone through. There are a lot of stupid, mean people out there who make decisions based on their ignorance."

"Well, you should tell anyone of that opinion they should go back to the barn and bugger their high horse. And besides, that would never happen around here," Mom asserts.

"Regardless, that's not why I don't want a death notice. It's just that it's none of their business. He's my son. It's our loss."

"Well, you can do what you want, dear. I just think it's the proper thing to do. I don't want to push you into anything you don't want to do."

"I'm feeling pushed."

"Sorry, Avie. That was honestly not my intention. I just brought it up because I thought it was something you hadn't thought about."

"Trust me, Mom. Death is on my mind pretty much constantly. No worries there."

CHAPTER 24

When the sun sets
and the moon awakens
Pictures reflect
pictures of you and me.
The lunar globe doesn't comprehend
that on glistening sand
we don't sit anymore.
But why do sunsets remind me of you?
And the clashing of waves beckons me to their grasp?
I sit and ponder of all we were through
and I wish I could tell you what the moon looks like
on black water.

I wrote this when I was in grade twelve. It's about a
boy I was in love with. We went to the beach with a group and

played in the water during the day. At night, we sauntered away from the crowded bonfire to kiss. I think I was infatuated with him for at least three weeks afterwards. I wonder where he is now. I wonder *who* he is now. What would have happened if we married and had children? Would my second child still have died? Do we have a predisposition in life towards specific tragedies and triumphs?

Are our lives written down before we're born in some celestial book and we have no choice to change the narrative? Or are we allowed to travel off the page at certain points, only to have the big events happen no matter what? Or is everything written in the sand, waiting to be constantly changed by the wind and the water? And where does God fit in here? Where does the power lie? Are we in charge of our destinies, or does God determine what happens?

Orrie, Duet and I went to church tonight for a Christmas service. I wasn't ready to go before now because I was afraid the minister would openly pray for me and I wouldn't be able to keep it together. There's nothing more dramatic and soulful than a bawling woman in the back seat. Despite my fears, everything goes well until we're leaving and gathering condolences.

> *"I heard about what happened, I'm so sorry."*
> *"Please come by someday if you want to talk."*
> *"I heard about your loss, if there's anything I can do ..."*
> *"How's Duet coping? Are you okay?"*

We plow through the concern and I keep my brave face on until a sour woman with blonde highlights clucks her head to the side and says it was God's will and he works in mysterious ways. God makes things happen for a reason.

"Is that what he told you?" I bite at her. "He never filled me in, but it's good to know my baby is better off without me."

Orrie apologizes and hurriedly corrals us out the door. By the time we get home, there are two messages from our minister. Maybe he wants to smooth things over. Maybe he isn't even aware of the event. All I know is that I'm not ready to talk to him yet.

Thank God for call display.

I know people mean well. I recognize people don't know what to say. There's nothing that will make everything okay. Nothing will ever be normal again and there's no magic sentence that can do the trick.

Kazam — there you go, Avril. No worries, my love. All good now.

That being said —

I know people mean well, but some comments really cut to the core. I never want to hear that this is for the best. I recognize the people who say these comments don't know any better, and that's a great thing. It's wonderful to be so blissfully unaware. Breath doesn't mean much until you realize you can't inhale. It's much better that people don't know what this is all about. I'm glad no one I know can empathize with me. I wish I didn't know what it was all about, either.

That being said —

Ignorance may be bliss, but it's also razor sharp to the jugular. If I hear *"At least you didn't go full term"* one more time, I'm either going to break down and bawl in front of them or ruthlessly murder the unsuspecting soothsayer. I carried Colin for 26 weeks. If he didn't have anencephaly and if I had spontaneously given birth, he could have survived with medical attention.

He was a baby.

He was born.

I gave birth to him.

He traveled down my birth canal and felt oxygen from the outside world.

He existed.

And now he doesn't exist.

But would it have been worse if all of this manifested a mere couple of months later? Holding him wouldn't have been more painful. Watching him dying wouldn't have hurt more if it had happened weeks later.

Ultimately, I guess I'm lying to people - I want everyone to know and feel what I went through. I want empathy. I don't want to be a good person who tries to make other people more comfortable with what's happened. I don't want to tell people I'm okay. That it's okay. That everything is okay. Because it isn't. Everything feels completely wrong in the world. I'm so lost and I'm finding it impossible to find my way back to myself. I have a dirty, sweaty handkerchief tightly strapped over my eyes and I can't see the use of it all. I'm completely terrified because nothing makes sense. I'm an adult who can't call for her mommy anymore. I'm too old and experienced to believe my mother can call off the monsters. I want to be three again. I want to look up to someone who can lie to me and tell me everything is okay. I need the lie. I need the religion of comfort. I need to fully believe that God is something more than an omniscient being who doesn't give a crap about what happens to me. I need him to care and to cry.

I feel like I'm the embodiment of contained chaos. I don't think I look like insanity personified, but I know for a fact that I currently don't have a grip on reality. I'm too aware of the fear factor. I am burdened with the knowledge things can indeed go wrong. I now know the power of a day. I know that within a short period of time, your entire existence can crack and burn. My saddest knowledge of all is the awakened awareness that things don't always work out for the best.

I want to be ignorant again.

I want bliss.

CHAPTER 25

It's been one week and two days since I last deliberately looked at Colin's card with his handprints and footprints. I had his card up on the mantle with all of the other Christmas and sympathy cards, but for some reason it felt morbid, so I put it up in my bedroom on the dresser. It just didn't feel right to have his handprints on display.

There's a part of me that feels guilty about keeping his prints out of public viewing, and then there's another part of me that wonders if this is just a part of moving on. But then yet another part of me wonders what is so great about moving on? The only way Colin exists is through memory, so if I stop thinking about him, am I killing him yet again? How is this healthy? In this instance, moving on means losing my child once again.

Orrie would say I'm being melodramatic. I've stopped confiding in him about thoughts such as these. He might get worried, and I don't need to feel guilty about that. I haven't even shared with him that my back hurts lately. I don't know if it is stress or exertion or what the heck is going on but I feel so sore. It's almost calming, though, to have physical pain. It gets my mind off my mind. I feel like the world is my potter, and I am a blob of wet clay that is being squished between its fingers.

Duet is having her nap now. I feel ashamed because she's at the point she doesn't need a nap anymore – actually she hasn't needed a nap for a while now. *I* impose her naptime now because *I* need her naptime. But even though I need it, it's awful when she's not around babbling and getting into mischief. There's nothing worse than being alone with a hollow brain where a vortex of nothingness resides. When Duet's running around my feet, I can fill my mind with her smiles and bright eyes. But when she's upstairs sleeping, it's so quiet and peaceful and horrid. I could turn on the TV but there's nothing of interest on. The television is even emptier than I am.

I have to get back on track. I have to get happy again on my own terms. I can't turn into someone who lives vicariously through my daughter. It's not fair to Duet and – even though I don't care at the moment – it's not fair to me.

There's so much freaking happiness around Christmas time that I'm beginning to feel like I'm doing something wrong by not feeling lovely and mushy. Maybe I should dress up like an elf and hang myself.

What made me chipper B.C. (Before Colin)? Happiness was being pregnant and looking forward to more children. Happiness was throwing up in the morning. Happiness was an expanding belly. Happiness was a cradle that was about to be filled after my belly emptied. Happiness was an illusion that was shattered by reality.

Okay, reframe. I have to concentrate on this. Think outside the box, Avril. I exist. Me. I am part of a unit, but I am my own entity. What makes me peppy inside my own existence?

Wine.

In all honesty, wine brings me joy. Sitting in a circle with a group of people while we have a couple glasses of red is great. Unfortunately, I don't think this is the healthiest solution right now, so I'll have to dig deeper than this. The last thing I need is to get tipsy and start spewing my depression to all my friends in the wee hours of the morning.

Yoga.

I could get back into yoga. Yoga is definitely more healthy than wine, but I think I'll have to wait a couple more weeks before I can do it again. According to the books, my body isn't ready for any physical activity outside of walking for a bit. I need to err on the side of karmic caution.

Playing.

Playing creates situations of pure delight. I need to play with Duet more. I want to escape to my youth when Joanie, the twins and I would create cocoons under blankets until our breath made everything so warm that we needed to lift the covers for air. I remember the distinct smells of little boy feet and Joanie's shampoo wafting about as we spent weekends building fortresses while Mom would gracefully navigate around all the chaos. Saturday evenings, we would all make mozzarella cheese pizza with hot dogs and afterwards, we would all sit together on the couch with our parents on either end, sandwiching us. Inevitably, the twins would fall asleep and we would take them upstairs to their room while mom and dad made cocktails and watched more television. I would happily go to sleep with the drone of the television downstairs gently coaxing me to drift off.

Actually –

I'm bored of looking for happiness. I'm too tired to be content. I think I'll sneak a few winks in while Duet is visiting dreamland. Sleep always makes me feel better.

Sleep.

Hmm ... is napping my first step to jubilance? Probably not, but it's a dreamy thought. If I could just have a deep, dreamless sleep, everything will start to sway back to being okay again. I don't even hope for awesome, just a simple movement towards anti-anxiety would be blissful at this point.

I can do this. I can become normal again. I did it before when times were challenging. I did it when Dad left. I did it when the twins left. I can do it again. Life has given me practice.

CHAPTER 26

"Can we wake up now?" Duet shouts in my ear.

"Are we awake?" I poke Orrie, whose head and shoulders are underneath a couple of pillows.

He rolls over. "I guess we are. What time is it?"

"It's time to get up," Duet bellows.

"It's 6:30," I protest.

"I guess it's time," Orrie decides, as if he had a choice in the matter.

Duet runs down the stairs, despite the fact I call after her to be careful. I put on my housecoat and look in the mirror. No Christmas photos of me this year. In addition to the fact that I'm still about fifteen – okay, twenty – pounds overweight, I look as pale as the ghost of Christmas past. I guess I still have to replace the blood that gushed out of me in the hospital. My eyes still look hollow, as well. Orrie comes up behind me and puts his arms around my waist. I quickly wriggle free before he can feel any unwanted lumps of flesh.

I give Orrie a peck on the cheek. "Do you want an omelet while we open the presents?"

"Maybe a muffin would be nice, if we have any," Orrie says as I gently push him away.

Duet yells from downstairs that we have to hurry, hurry, hurry. We both holler back that we're coming. She runs up the stairs and grabs onto my housecoat to hasten the procession. "You won't believe what I got, Mommy! You just won't believe it!"

Orrie and I ooh and ahh over Duet's booty from Santa. She races back and forth from the stocking to show us every present he brought. "This is the car I wanted, Daddy. It's the pink one with the hearts on it. It'll take the dolls anywhere they want to go. How can he know, Daddy? How come he's so smart? How can he know what I wanted?" She stops for a second, looking a bit concerned. "He can't read my brain, can he?"

"No," Orrie laughs. "He just has good sense. Good sense is a treasure. Remember that."

"Pirates have treasure, Daddy. Not Santa."

"Ah, yes. My mistake."

Duet looks longingly at the Christmas tree. "Are we ready to open the presents from people yet?"

I shake my head. "Nope, we have to have breakfast first."

We go to the kitchen where Duet impatiently scoffs down her cereal, sending dirty looks at us while we eat our toast like civilized people. *Don't you care?* I can tell she's thinking. "Can't you hurry?" She says out loud.

Orrie and I give up halfway through our coffees and decide to bring our cups out to the living room where we can drink in peace, if not quiet. I can't help thinking next Christmas will be even emptier than this one. Next Christmas was supposed to be one with both Duet and Colin. If everything had worked out properly, I would still be pregnant this Christmas and next year Colin would be crawling through the wrapping paper. My eyes start to water so I take a big sip of coffee to hide them.

"You okay?" Orrie murmurs.

"Yeah, I'm just thinking about what next year was supposed to be like."

Orrie tightly squeezes my hand. "It can still be like that."

"It will never be the same."

"Well, there's still the possibility of a baby next Christmas," Orrie whispers so Duet can't hear.

"I don't want to replace Colin, Orrie."

"That's not what I was saying."

"I know. Let's just open the presents and forget about it. Merry Christmas, Orrie. I really mean that."

"It can only get better, Avie."

"I know. I love you."

"I love you too."

We hang out by the tree for another hour or so and then start to clean up the wrapping paper and boxes. I have a nice, long bubble bath with luxurious products from Orrie. Eventually, we start to get ready for Christmas dinner and visitors.

"I'll be down in a minute," I tell Orrie from the top of the stairs. "Just keep cooking dinner without me."

"Is everything okay?" Orrie frowns. "Your mom and Joanie will be here soon."

"Yes, of course," I smile. "I just want to get changed. My pants feel too tight and I'm uncomfortable."

"Okay," Orrie answers, reassured.

I go to my bedroom, changing my pants so I can hide the real reason I'm up here. I want to open Colin's present while it's still Christmas, and I can't do that if Orrie or Duet are around.

While we were Christmas shopping, I saw a little red stocking cap that was so tiny it barely fit around my fist. I hid from Orrie long enough to purchase it. It has a gentle green pom-pom that's made from some sort of synthetic fiber too soft to even be imagined. I bought it on the spot and in secret. I took it home, immediately hiding it underneath the bed where no one would find it. I need to give something to my son this Christmas. For some reason, I need this ritual.

I take out the present, feigning surprise. "Oh, how pretty," I whisper, without even feeling silly. "Do you want to see it?" I lift my eyes to the ceiling. "Yes?" I open the present, taking the little hat out to place on my lap. "This is for you, Colin. This is from your Mommy. I'm your Mommy and I love you very much. I wish you could be here, baby. I wish it so much. You're not here - not physically. But I hope you know you'll always be with me. I miss you even though you are forever inside my heart. Merry Christmas, Colin."

I take the cap, kissing it before I tuck it in a pocket of a jacket I don't wear very often at the back of my closet. I want this to be close to me. I take it out again to smell it, even though I know it doesn't even smell like him. I want him here, but that's not possible, so I'm going to settle for a soft little red and green hat. That has to be enough for now.

As I finally put the hat away, I hear Duet's muffled wail to hurry up because they need my help in the kitchen. She then bumbles up the stairs as Orrie unsuccessfully tries to get her to stay downstairs. I open the door and she wraps her arms around my legs. "Mommy, you need to do the carrots. Daddy never gets them right." She looks desperately at me. "And he was going to use canned peas," she whispers. "You don't like it when he does that."

I laugh as I lift her up. "But Daddy likes canned peas better. Maybe we should let him have his way, just this once."

She sighs. "If you say so …"

"But we'll make regular peas for the rest of us. How does that sound?"

"Good. Let's do that. It's good to make everyone happy. Especially at Christmas, right?"

"Right."

"Can I say grace?" Duet asks. "It's a special occasion."

"Sure, sweetie. Do you know what you're going to say?"

"I'm going to say thank you. God is good to us. I want to thank him."

My eyes tear up a bit and I pretend to sneeze. "Yes, he is. There's a lot to be thankful for."

"I'm thankful for you, I'm thankful for Daddy, I'm thankful for Auntie Joanie, I'm thankful for Gramma, I'm thankful for my room …" Duet continues her litany of appreciation as we go down the hallway towards the stairs. Once we get to the bottom, I turn her on my hip so she's facing me.

"I'm thankful for you, Du," I whisper as our noses touch. "I love you so much. You are the most awesome daughter in the world."

"And you're the best mommy. And Daddy is the best daddy. And Auntie Joanie is the best auntie …" She continues her list as she wiggles away from me to help Orrie with his peas. A wave of true appreciation washes over me as I watch the two of them. I am lucky. I have to concentrate on that. That's my ladder. I look up, giving a very quick prayer of thanks. *Thanks for this, God. I still don't understand the other, but I'm grateful for this.*

CHAPTER 27

It's the end of February. I'm drinking expired eggnog and eating the last of the Valentine's Day chocolates as I zone out in front of my television. I spit out a metal candy wrapper, disgusted that everyone on the screen looks shiny and new like they just stepped out of their L.A. packaging. None of them seem real. Even the ones going through challenges look dewy fresh. In real life, people who have it tough are more wrinkled than the carefree lot. I always assumed it was the stress that furrowed their faces, but now I know better. It's the whacked out space/time continuum that warps a person's appearance. The past few weeks have been more like seventy years in real time. I've dealt with more intense thoughts and experiences than are possible to contain in mere months. I should be a centenarian by now.

Life gets in the way of life. Specific activities build pathways that lead to completely unfathomable consequences. Conversations can create a mood that is amenable to sex. Sex at the right moment can create a sentient being. Something as simplistic as not taking the right vitamin can keep life from progressing in your womb. But not doing anything is taking a stance, as well. Not having the conversations, or cultivating those relationships can result in a potentially safer existence, but ultimately a less tolerable one. I wonder about the night Colin was conceived. Was there something in my subconscious that told me I should claim a headache and just stay quiet under the covers? If I had watched a movie that night and gone to bed after Orrie went to sleep, would my life be okay? Would my wrinkles vanish?

There are women out there who are proud of their wrinkles. They show character. Mine don't – they show the ravages of life. Is character pain? If someone has a completely carefree life, are they devoid of personality? Is it a bad thing to be innocent and beautiful? I'm only 32. I should be just beginning the journey of adulthood. The roaring twenties are part of my past. Now is the time to buckle down and get serious. Well, I'm definitely serious. I haven't laughed for many days (thirteen years in real time).

Does guilt cause wrinkles? Everything is about guilt lately. Sometimes I feel guilty about still being alive ...

which leads to ...

feeling guilty about wanting to die ...

which leads to ...

feeling guilty about not wanting to die.

I'm becoming scared of leaving the house. Each time I venture out increases the chance I'll meet up with people who don't know what happened. How will they react when I tell them I lost my baby? Lost. I lost my baby. It's like I unintentionally left him behind at the supermarket. *"Where's Colin?"* *"Oh, darn, I think he's in the dairy aisle at the grocery store. I'm pretty sure he's somewhere between the cheddar and the kosher dills. Will you go try to find him? I'm busy preparing supper."*

Will people think I did something wrong? Did I do something wrong? And why should I be concerned about other people? Shouldn't I be thinking about Colin's departure and not about what other people think? What kind of a mother am I? I'm a bad mother for losing my son. I'm bad enough that he's not around. How could that possibly be good? How can good be part of this awful picture? There's nothing good about it. There certainly couldn't have been a worse outcome.

Guilt is good. Feeling guilty is proper. I have to feel guilty because that means I'm a good mother. If I feel blameless, then I must be an unfeeling beast who never deserved to be pregnant in the first place. My guilt is atonement – the loss isn't enough. But if guilt is good, do I deserve to feel guilty? If feeling bad is making me feel good, then where's the lesson? Where's the punishment?

I'm beginning to recognize the look of people who know about Colin. They ask me how I'm doing like there's a droplet of bitter lemon on their top lip. Some of them even appear to have onion blowing in their eyes and they squint while they ask. All in all, it's a puckering motion that takes over the entire face.

So, how's it going?

So, what's my response?

I have a standard answer of *"I'm doing okay,"* nodding thoughtfully as I respond. This is usually enough to forestall any further questions. I have to ensure I put a lot of stress on the word "doing." For some reason, this is a key factor in the equation. The nodding is pretty important, as well. This seems to make people believe me, and they leave reassured that I'm coping up to their standards.

So what do I tell those poor, unsuspecting people who have no idea what happened? *How are you doing? I haven't seen you in a while. What are you up to?"* Can I get away with saying *"Nothing, and you?"* Am I allowed to? Or am I expected to tell people the events of the past couple months? Would they like to know? Which response makes me a bad person? Which proves I'm unbalanced? Society has collectively agreed that the phrase "how are you" doesn't even mean anything anymore. It's pretty much equivalent to "hello." No one expects any answer other than "fine." People actually get annoyed if you go on a long diatribe about how you really are. It's neither expected nor wanted. I feel safe and enveloped in this concept. This can be my protection.

I turn off the television, collecting Duet to go grocery shopping. We drive to the store that has the kiddie cart that's way too small for her. She really loves it, so I haven't stopped using it. I'll wait until she can't fit in it any longer and then we'll deal with it. At some point I'm going to have to stop putting things off, but not yet. I'll work on that later. It can be a new year's resolution for next year. I'm currently working on other things.

I zone out for a bit as I push my cart around at the grocery store. I wonder how the woman checking out the lettuce is. How's she doing? If I were in the know about what's going on in her life, would I pucker up my face before asking how she is? What's the state of her being, anyway? She doesn't look depressed, but then again, I probably don't either. Am I depressed? I honestly haven't thought about it lately. I guess that means I'm not. Or does it? Am I?

I'm honestly trying to function.

I'm trying to do the laundry.

I'm trying to do the dishes.

I'm trying to fill out insurance forms.

I'm trying to answer the phone.

I'm trying to watch television.

I'm trying to pretend to be normal for Duet.

I'm trying to brush my hair.

I'm trying to shower so I don't smell.

I'm trying to make the bed.

I'm trying to clean up so my housekeeper won't know how much of a mess my life is in.

I'm trying.

I'm not going to live a fearful life. I'm not going to go crazy. I just won't. And if I do, I'll find a way to disguise it so no one will be the wiser. I'll go to Switzerland to get the best plastic surgery Orrie's money can buy to erase my wrinkles, eradicating all my struggles. No one will ever see my pain. It's mine and I don't have to share it if I don't want to.

CHAPTER 28

It's a beautiful wintery Saturday so Joanie and I decide to take Duet to the playground by Joanie's apartment building. I brought some blankets to cover us up while we sit at a picnic table watching Duet run around. We're both silent, taking in the elated screams of the kids. Their voices seem louder in the crisp air. I forcefully exhale so I can see my cloudy breath.

"Am I good people?" I ask Joanie out of the blue.

"What do you mean?" she asks. "Of course you are."

I look over to ensure Duet is still safely playing on the swings. "I suppose I am," I reflect as I blow into my cup of steaming hot latte. "So why? Why did this happen to me? Why did Colin die? Why do bad things happen to good people? Why?"

Joanie quickly looks around at the other mothers and caregivers to ensure no one is listening to our conversation. Everyone seems to be talking to each other or otherwise ignoring us. "Why are you asking? Is everything okay?"

"Why? Why wouldn't I ask this? Why do good people wonder what the heck is going on? Do bad people wonder? Do bad people care?"

Joanie takes my hands in hers. "Avie, are you okay? You're not acting normal. What can I do?"

I smirk. "Of course I'm okay. I'm just messed up, that's all. Nothing to worry about."

Joanie moves in a bit closer. "Is Orrie helping out? Have you talked to Orrie about this?"

"No, he doesn't want to talk about it. It's so weird."

"Well, you were kind of the same way when Dad left. You just pretended everything was normal."

"How did any of us deal with Dad abandoning us? It was so sudden and awkward." I shiver and tighten the scarf around my neck. "I don't even remember specific details, just that you drank a lot, Mom became overprotective, and the twins wanted to distance themselves from all of us. Did we handle it well?"

Joanie stares at the ground. "Probably. Maybe not. Well, no, I guess not. But who gets graded on these things? Life isn't perfect, Avie. You can't pretend it is, or try to make it perfect, because you'll always end up being disappointed." She looks up at me. "Life is awesome and scary and lovely and horrible, but it is never binary. It is everything all of the time. Not good or bad and all that rot."

"But I want to find a reason for Colin dying. I need to."

"You're not going to," Joanie says gently. "Sometimes there are no reasons. Bad things and good things just happen."

"I want there to be order. I always did. That's why I became a lawyer. I was passionately going to change lives. I was going to make things better. I was going to be the red streak in this blue world. I was going to create balance through measures of justice."

"But then you ended up not liking the law." Joanie lovingly punches my shoulder, trying to lighten the mood.

I lean into her fist, and she curls her hand around my bicep and squeezes. "Yep. Also, I was a good lawyer, but not great. I wasn't going to make my mark in the world. Things would change for better or for worse without me."

"That's depressing." Joanie pulls a cigarette from a silver case in her purse and reaches for her lighter. I widen my eyes, gesturing towards Duet, so she tucks them back into her purse.

I nod at her. "But then something amazing came along – a night without protection and Duet was conceived. At first I was wary about being a mother, do you remember?"

"Wary?" Joanie whoops. "Well, that's minimizing things. You were totally freaked out. You were in the middle of that big project."

"Yep. I remember wondering how I could give up my career even though I hated it. I knew I wanted to be a mother someday; I just wasn't sure if the time was right. I hadn't left a mark on the world yet. But each day of being pregnant with Duet was a dream. I was never sick, and being tired wasn't a burden. I loved my body while I was pregnant. Going on the scale and not worrying about gaining weight was enough to make me ecstatic." We're both silent for a moment, watching Duet play. "I had finally found my niche in life," I rest my head on Joanie's shoulder. "I found what I was actually good – no, make that superb – at. I was even at the point of worrying that it would be a letdown after she was born, because everything was going so well."

Joanie skootches closer beside me, wrapping the blanket around us. "Well, that was a needless concern. Duet is the best thing to ever happen to any of us."

"I know, right? I don't just love Duet; I'm in love with her. Everything she does is amazing and when she smiles, I melt with joy. In my head, I used to attribute some of her loveliness to my parenting skills. She excelled because I was an excellent mother."

"You are an exceptional mother," Joanie soothes.

I start to cry. I'm grateful my sunglasses will hide my tears. "And now that feeling has changed, somehow. I no longer feel like the perfect mother. And that loss hurts almost as much as losing Colin. I failed at being a mother to Colin because something happened to him while my body was taking care of him. That doesn't happen to perfect mothers. And now I question my parenting skills with Duet each day. I wonder how I'm going to break her. I wonder what decisions I'll make that will harm her, and that scares me because I owe her so much."

"Avie, you weren't the perfect mother before, and you aren't now. You are never going to be. You're going to be the best mother you can. No one is capable of perfection, and that's okay."

"Perfection is protection," I argue. "It keeps you safe."

Joanie grabs my shoulders. "No it doesn't. But trying to be perfect keeps you from being happy. It's about trying to be a better person, not a perfect person. And it's about being graceful when things get mucked up. Perfection is a burden. Go for grace."

"When I first had Duet, I felt this conviction to become a better person," I sniff, wiping my nose on the back of my glove. "I felt so wholesome."

"That sounds good. Keep going for that," Joanie encourages.

"The pre-Duet me would go through my personal history, thinking of all the mistakes I've ever made in my life. There were some things I merely cringed over, but quite a few were enough to make me want to drive off the road with embarrassment."

Joanie shakes her head. "That sounds pretty unhealthy."

"I know. But post-Duet, I came to the conclusion that there's not too much I can do about these mistakes except learn from them and go on. They are only detrimental if they are repeated over and over. Mistakes can create good."

"You're going back and forth, here. I'm getting confused. How do you feel now?"

"Now I am going through every mistake I've ever made, desperately searching why this happened to me. Life not being fair just isn't enough. I must have done something to deserve this punishment. You get what you give in life."

"Avie …" Joanie starts but I am just ramping up.

"What did I give to get this? Or is it more like life's great balancing act? Something to create equality in one's personal universe? Were things so great with Duet that I needed to be brought down a notch? What if it's not about balance? What if life is one big cesspool of chaos? Does that make me feel better somehow?"

I'm snotty, teared out, and have a bit of a headache. I look around to see if anyone started watching us, but no one is even remotely bothered. Crisis to the left, swings and slides to the right. Life goes on without noticing. We could just as easily be talking about the weather for all anyone could care. I consciously try to listen to other people's conversations, but I'm not able to hear anything except the occasional squeal from the kids in the playground. I hope Duet doesn't stop playing for a while. I don't want her to see me crying.

Joanie is silent for a moment. "Well, I don't know if it will make you feel any better, but I officially don't believe in karma. In my world, it's scientifically debunked. I even have the perfect example for you. Last week, I got a phone call from my friend, Lisa. She wanted me to come over because her car needed a boost. Do you remember Lisa? The one who divorced the dodgy art dealer from down south? Of course, I told her I'd be right over. But along the way, my car ran over a nail so I had to phone a tow truck."

"That sucks, but what does that have to do with karma?"

"Shouldn't my tire have busted if I was on my way to commit a felony, or something less philanthropically inclined? I can't believe the favor I couldn't even perform cost me a new tire. If I had been a jerk and told Lisa I was too busy, I would have been sipping coffee on my deck during rush hour instead of paying good money to a guy covered in grease."

"But in order for it to be scientifically proven, doesn't the experiment have to replicate itself over and over again?" I quip. "Besides, karma works to balance things already accomplished in the past rather than acts or works in progress."

Joanie dismisses me as she takes a sip of her coffee, "It happens all the time. This is just one example."

"Well, on the plus side, if you truly don't believe in karma, you can use your story as fodder for the next person who tries to talk to you about it," I suggest. "But without karma, I guess the downside is there's no balance in the universe."

"Screw balance. People blindly think balance is a positive aspect to life, but balance isn't necessarily the cat's meow. True balance has horrific consequences. Pure balance means that every moment of ecstasy generates an unfounded tragedy. For every innocent birth, there's a senseless murder. For every tit, there's a tat. For every good intention, there's a sharp nail in my tire. Balance sucks. Officially. Life would be so much better without balance. Life would be happier. Life would be more secure."

I stand up, kicking my legs to get the blood pumping. "But it almost feels that without karma or fairness, life seems so meaningless. There's no recipe for making things right. I want a script. There has to be fairness in the world. There has to be something to hold on to. I almost think it would be preferable that I did something to deserve this, rather than a random twist of fate."

"Who says what's fair?" Joanie ponders as she looks up at the clouds. "Is fairness just a beneficial personal outcome? What if there is a true cosmic consciousness and experience out there?"

"I'm not following you."

"What if there is a yin and a yang that exists globally? If so, then life is truly balanced and karmic and fair - but it's *all* life, not just yours and mine." Joanie pulls the blanket closer. "What if the gives and gets are global? Am I sentenced to a cosmic payment for a heinous deed that Raymond, from Cincinnati, committed?"

"If so – screw you, Cincinnati Raymond. I'm going to hate you forever." I emphatically slap my knee, trying to lighten the mood. Duet is probably going to want to leave soon.

Joanie playfully shakes her fist. "And I hope Jenny from Toronto does something that makes you pay dearly."

We lightly chuckle and start to gather our things so we're closer to the swings. "Well, this is a conversation Orrie would really get into. I'll need to include you the next time I try to talk to him about this."

"You need to talk about this with Orrie."

I look around the playground, my vision a little foggy from my steamed-up sunglasses. "I know. But let's not talk about that now."

After we drop Joanie off, I go through a drive-thru for coffee to kill some time. Duet is passed out in her car seat so it's better if I drive around to let her nap for a bit. I wonder what Duet thinks about. Is it all about the next adventure? Do kids need meaning or do they just crave experience? I turn on the radio to pass the time, but then turn it off to think about my conversation with Joanie. How does everything we talked about today work with God? Does this work with God? If so, does God judge or bless us as a collective or as an individual? Are individuals sometimes the collateral damage of a collective judgment?

Does God care? Caring and consequence are two separate subject matters. I use my analytical tweezers to distinguish the two: God can care, but horrific things can happen even though he cares about it. God can be sad about bad things happening.

So – next question – if God cares, why doesn't he do something about it? I mean, he's all powerful, right? He can part seas and burn bushes, right? He sent down a Savior for all humankind, right?

But what if this whole experience is about more than what's happening right now? What if everything that happens to us right now is a test for what is about to come? What if this life is not just about this lifetime? What if it's about something with a grander scheme? What if it's all about what happens after we don't exist on this plane? What if it is more than the now, more than the possible century that we have on this planet? What if it's of more consequence? What if Colin already passed the true test in his infancy? Is that not a gift? What if (if) everything that happens – good, bad, whatever – is just an ultimate evaluation of how we deal with a situation? What if (if) the ninety plus years we are on this planet is just a preliminary contest as to how we will truly be blessed or damned? If (if) that's so – and if (if) Colin's already won the contest, how am I faring? What (if)? Does that kill the why? And if so, does that make me feel better?

Next existential question - if that makes me feel better, does that make everything a bit better, even if it isn't perfect?

CHAPTER 29

I'm beginning to think I exist so everyone else can get their priorities straight. No one is allowed to complain around me anymore. When someone is about to sound off about a petty situation and they just fleetingly think about me, they count their blessings and get on with the day in a new light.

Nothing like a personal tragedy to put other people's lives in perspective. I remember a poem I read in grade ten or eleven. It was about a little boy who died in a tractor accident. All of the other kids were totally excited to tell their parents about it because they knew it'd make their parents treasure them all the more. Or at least that's how I remember it.

I was at the store with Duet the other day and a woman came up to us. She patted me on the head – I swear, she actually patted me on my head – and told me everything was going to be okay.

"Thank you," I replied. I had no idea who this woman was.

"We're all praying for you, dear."

"Thanks. This is Duet, my daughter."

"She's doing well?"

"Yep. She's perfect."

"That's good, dear. It's good for you to know you can do it right."

I honestly would have belted her if she wasn't around eighty and wasn't trying to be nice. As it was, I awkwardly told her I am indeed pleased with "doing it right" at least once.

I'm not even shocked with people anymore. I've learned that having something horrible happen makes you other people's property. I have become a celebrity of doom.

"Oh, there's that girl who lost the baby."

"The one who had the miscarriage?"

"Apparently it wasn't a miscarriage, actually. I heard the baby had no head."

[Gasp] "No head?"

"Yes, it's terrible. I wonder what it looked like. Do you think she saw the baby?"

"I can't imagine. The doctors probably wouldn't allow it. Shhh, she's coming."

"Pretty little thing. It's such a shame, huh?"

I am at your service. Please feel free to feel better.

CHAPTER 30

None of us talk about Dad anymore. It's like he's a dream that we have collectively forgotten. Joanie and I chat about everything except our father. Mom tries to bring him up, but I always find ways to distract her because it's never an enjoyable conversation. I wonder if the twins talk about him when they get together in exotic bars or on tennis courts.

Am I angry with my father for leaving? Do I think he was selfish for doing so? Am I mad that he viewed each of us inconsequential enough to puff away on a jet stream of exhaust to new lands and other adventures? Does he have a new family now? Is that why we don't count? My dad left before any of his children were fully formed. He abandoned his daughters before he could give us away at the altar.

I think there were obvious indicators that Dad was going to leave. We grew up with a rigid police officer for a father who metamorphosed into something entirely different after retirement. Joanie and I were convinced that something happened on one of his cases that concretely changed him. Or maybe that just made us feel better. He never spoke about his work, even to Mom, so we have no evidence of this. There's no trail to investigate. He simply turned into a different person, and then our father became a ghost. He didn't want to be known as "Dad" anymore, so we started calling him Harold. When she felt it was appropriate to say so, Mom told me she was sure he was seeing other women, but he wouldn't admit to any wrongdoing. Then again, she also told me he argued that there was nothing wrong with stepping out with the ladies. Dad had a way with words that Mom didn't, so she never won any arguments. He stopped going to church and was quite critical of anyone who chose to attend, including Mom. This made Mom want to go even more, so the cracks began to widen. Joanie, the twins and I weren't sure what to do. It didn't feel like it was our business. It was Mom and Dad's issue, not ours.

Then, all of a sudden, Dad (or rather, Harold) moved out of our childhood home, never to speak to any of us again. We got postcards sent to the proper addresses here and there, but that was it. We think he is alive, but that is it. We have a father from memory. That will be it.

I almost wish I had inherited Dad's power of disconnection. Then I could instantly forget about Colin and feel whole again. Actually, no. What I really want are memories of Colin without sadness. I want to remember this happened, and not feel bitter or wronged about it. He will always be with me. I just don't want to be fearful of that prospect.

I don't have much luck with men in my family. My brothers and my father all left me. My son left me. The only ones remaining from my bloodline are female. We stick together, eat together, and annoy each other, all while being within a close physical and emotional distance. Why did all my men leave? Will Orrie leave? He's not a blood relative; does this protect me from abandonment?

I met Orrison Bale at a high school dance. It was my crimson period – my hair was dyed deep red, similar to the color of healthy blood. I was seventeen and annoyed that I was a carbon copy of everyone else. We all had our own thoughts and emotions, so why did we all look the same? So – I dyed my hair. And I was naive enough to think that made me distinct. But I didn't want to go too far in being different. I appreciated that people were finally not talking about Dad leaving us anymore; it was becoming normalized. I didn't want to trigger anything explosive by being too divergent.

High school was such a strange time – things that don't seem very important now were monumental then. And because of what happened with my father, I tried to make anything monumental seem inconsequential to keep the panic attacks at bay. *Yes, my father left us. So? Doesn't that happen to everyone at some point?* But I think things that weren't a huge issue ended up hurting me even more than the things that should have broken me. I remember a girl, Connie, said something rude about me in front of a group of people in the cafeteria. It completely devastated me. I went home that night and cried in Mom's lap for over two hours – way more tears than when Dad left. Joanie beat Connie up the next day and was suspended for a week. I told Mom I didn't expect Joanie to hurt someone. Mom gave me a quick kiss on the top of my head and curtly advised that I should never apologize for having emotions. She said not to worry about Joanie, either. Everything would work out. I believed her. But while I hoped everything was going to be okay, I was so jealous of most of the kids in my class who seemingly had immaculate, perfect lives.

Orrie was from another school and came to our dance with an acquaintance of mine. He was cute, tall and mysterious, but I never really paid much attention to him after the initial buzz of looking at a new male in the crowd. We all got together at a party after the dance. That's when I found out he was going to the same university as I was. We started hanging out during Frosh week, but we never dated until we were both in law school. By then we were best friends who had unwittingly been in love for years. Our goal was to get married, have a couple of kids, and live happily ever after. Cut to the present: we're still living, so the ever after has yet to come.

Orrie is my soul mate, but would I have married him if I knew what the outcome would be? Would I sacrifice all of the good (great) times we've had in order to save myself from the pain of losing Colin? Could I sacrifice Duet's existence? If I never knew what it was like to hold her, would I miss not ever having her? Would I have other children to fill the void?

No.

A thousand times never. No, no, no.

But is Duet's life worth Colin's death?

I feel guilty even asking these questions. How can I even process these thoughts when I can hear Duet breathing beside me? How can I love her, yet think about never having her?

But how can I deal with never having Colin? Am I dealing? Is asking questions like this dealing, or is this another one of those unhealthy thought processes I'm supposed to be suppressing? Does a good mother even think about never having her child?

I run over to where Duet is playing with her dolls. I grab her, squeezing so tight there is a danger of her peeing on me.

"What's wrong, mommy?"

"Nothing, Du. Mommy just loves you."

"Are you okay?"

"I think I'm getting there."

"What?" she asks, her eyes wide and innocent.

"Of course I'm okay," I lie.

But I'm getting closer to telling the truth.

CHAPTER 31

Orrie and I are at the concession stand waiting to get snacks for a romantic comedy. The smell of popcorn is making me a drooling mess. Orrie tells me what to order before he takes a quick bathroom break. He figures the line is long enough that he'll be back before we get to the cash. I'm debating whether to get a large or extra-large combo when Samantha, a former colleague, weaves in behind me. After we talk about the weather and which movie we're here to see, Samantha tells me about her promotion at work. "Plus I'm meeting my new boyfriend here."

I smile. "That's exciting."

She leans in, whispering, "He's pretty hot, if I do say so myself." She winks and starts to giggle but then a horrified look takes over her face. "Avril, I'm so sorry. I didn't mean to go on like that."

"Like what?" I honestly don't know what she is talking about.

"You know, raving on about how good I have it. It's so distasteful. I'm really sorry. I never even thought."

"Thought what?" I ask, still clueless.

"Well, after everything that's been going on with you, I shouldn't be rubbing your nose in my life."

"You're not rubbing my nose in anything," I respond, slowly. "You're just telling me what's going on. I haven't talked to you in a bit. We're just catching up."

"Thanks, that's very kind of you."

I feel the anger starting to churn in my chest. "It's not nice. I'm not being generous."

"Yes, yes. I'm sorry."

"Stop being sorry."

"Okay, sorry. I mean – you know," she stumbles, biting her lip.

I move ahead in the line, then turn back to look her squarely in the eyes. "I'm not a sympathy case."

"I never meant to imply that. Maybe I should just go. Everything I'm saying is coming out wrong."

I deflate like a balloon. "No, stay." I put my hand on her arm. "I'm sorry. You're not saying anything wrong."

We pretend to talk a bit longer until things get too uncomfortable to keep going. Orrie finally returns, giving me a reason to officially conclude the conversation. I'm sure I'll connect with her in a couple of weeks and everything will be fine. It's just weird knowing that friends who I used to burp in front of are now watching what they say around me. I feel like I've done something unforgivable to ruin our friendship. No one knows how to deal with me anymore. I'm cursed and they don't want me to rub off on them. *Don't get too close to Avril or your kids will die.*

It's not that I require people to be jealous of my existence, but I certainly don't desire to be viewed as pathetic. I don't want people to feel sorry for me. It's not just a pride factor. It's the reality that I honestly do have a great life. Even though Colin died, I'm not completely afflicted and unfortunate. At least I don't think I am. Or more to the point, at least I don't think so all of the time.

Just make sure you don't accidentally touch me.
You'll catch me.

You don't want to be it.

CHAPTER 32

There is a huge thunderstorm outside and lightning must have struck gold somewhere. I don't like it when the power is off; it's too eerily quiet. The silence of the house is deafening. There's no electrical humming or vapid television to dull the parts of my imagination where the dark thoughts live and thrive. When the outside illumination is dead, the chisel chips away at the container of the darkness so it can escape and let loose.

> Whatever doesn't kill you makes you stronger.
> Whatever doesn't kill you makes you stronger.
> Whatever doesn't kill you makes you stronger.

Ah, the necessary chants of life. Such a statement doesn't mean much until you come to a point where you are almost murdered by pain. After that, you're so weak it's impossible to feel anything but breakable. It's like there's an eternal fracture in your life just waiting to crack wide open, never to be repaired. The future doesn't necessarily look bleak, but it will never be promising.

Am I getting stronger?

I'm alive. That's a step.

Have I ever wanted to stop going? Even if I search throughout the darkest crevices and shadows of my brain, I know I always wanted to survive this for Duet. I am the mother of two children – one I can hold in my arms, the other I hold in my heart. Colin is dead, so he can't get stronger. I survived, so I have to. Am I experiencing some type of maternal survivor's guilt? Does such a psychological condition even exist? I'm sure there's a psychologist out there somewhere who has latched onto it at some point.

"Hi folks, we're here to talk to Dr. Avril Bale about her newest book: Survival Guilt: A Mother's Perspective. *Dr. Bale, what led you to your discovery of this unique condition?"*

From my dark bedroom, I pretend to look at the camera and mentally respond to the fake talk show host:

"Well, it's a personal discovery, Bethany. You see, I had a baby who died of anencephaly. Or, I guess he had anencephaly so he died. Maybe I'll write a book on that theory next week: which came first, the death or the anencephaly? It's a chicken-or-egg kind of debate. But I ramble. Basically, I have no idea what I'm talking about. I have no clue about anything anymore. I figure I should share my psychological disorder with the world because that's what people do now. We share pain with each other. Pain doesn't exist until you sit on a talk show, telling strangers your most intimate thoughts and fears. It's the new way of dealing. Poets used to do it, now talk show guests do."

It's around two in the morning and I'm lying in bed next to Orrie, desperately trying to keep my breath in tune with his so I can soothe myself to sleep, but there's no use. I'm destined to be alone with my thoughts for the next couple of hours.

I try to think of white, fluffy sheep bouncing happily over fences in Scotland. Instead, I think of the time I was at my cousin's farm in springtime when a new crop of lambs were bursting out of their mothers' bellies. One was breech and my cousin's stepdad let me stick my arm into the amniotic fluid to feel its hoof. I wasn't particularly excited about the prospect of doing so, but I wasn't going to be a girl about it. Being a girl was not a cool thing to be on a farm, especially a couple of decades ago. That particular lamb lived, but others didn't. The ones that didn't survive the birth canal were fed to the pigs, while the cats ate the afterbirth of both the surviving and dead lambs. I can still hear the cats licking the red, gooey mess in the corner of the barn and I will always remember what a lamb's birth smells like among the tang of manure, wood and straw.

I flash back to the present to consider my own birthing. What if I am passing along the wrong DNA? What if all the goodness in me was passed down to Duet so I have nothing left to give? Should I have more children? Am I capable of being a proper parent to more than one child? Am I actually a good parent for Duet? Do I just assume so because it would hurt too much to think otherwise?

I know Duet will always love me – that's the easy emotion between mother and child. When Duet was born, I felt this huge new bond with my mother because I realized the depth of a mother's love. I remember talking about mother/child relationships with friends before I had children. It's so much easier when it's all a theory. You can stand back as an expert, quoting trendy psychologists of the week. It's fun because you don't have anything invested in it.

I envision a television talk show from the future. The set is decorated in Styrofoam plus ample brassy fabrics. There's a jingle rambling on in the background while a woman with big breasts flops around with a microphone.

Duet:

The worst thing is that even though I love my mother, I have no respect for her. This leads to all sorts of problems. She has no life of her own. She has always sucked on to everyone else's accomplishments. This, added to her martyr complex - she would be more accomplished if it wasn't for her giving so much all this time - makes her a huge pill to swallow.

CUT TO AUDIBLE GASP FROM AUDIENCE.

Duet:

Yeah, it got worse over the years. Last week, I went over to her house for coffee. I feel it's important to see my family quite frequently – family is important even if your mother is a freak. I just wish she was easier to deal with ... Anyway, instead of a nice bonding experience, I left with a nervous stomach because I had a huge fight with her over the price of domestic automobiles.

CUT TO LOOK OF SYMPATHY FROM AUDIENCE.

Duet:

That's all it takes. I went over to visit one time when she was up all night working on dad's laundry. She didn't have any sleep because she doesn't just launder clothes, she irons every piece of underwear that comes out of the dryer. I am of the opinion she only irons so she can complain about it, but that's my disrespect coming through. So — she offered me a ham sandwich. I said sure, I would love one. I then realized it was a canned ham sandwich, so I declined. No big deal. I don't like canned ham so I didn't want a sandwich. In any other household, that would be the end of things but Mother became offended because I thought I was too good for canned ham. She went through all the bother of making a sandwich — you know, she risked the onslaught of botulism if she cut her hand on the lid — and I didn't even want it.

CUT TO LOOK OF HORROR FROM AUDIENCE.

Duet:

Yeah, she's a strange one, all right. She worries about everything. I wasn't even allowed to play after dusk because I might get bitten by a mosquito. I won't even get started on her sun/UV issues ...

147

I shudder off the image and the fear of what Duet might say about me in the future. Everything is correct except the bit about canned ham. I would never give my child canned ham, it's too salty.

I turn my body over in the bed to escape the fake cameras and the non-existent bright lights. I stare down the hallway towards the bathroom. The house starts humming again, letting me know the power has come back on. Maybe I'll have a bath. A clean recovery might be just what I need. I just have to be quiet so I don't wake Orrie. It isn't normal to have a bath this late.

I run the tub, stirring smelly oils into the hot water. The middle of the night is actually a great chance to just sit back and soak. I let my mind relax, trying to concentrate on the heat and the smell of the steam. My mind wanders to the fact that I don't know what Colin's whole head looked like. I never really thought about that until now. I will never have an idea what his whole little head looked like. *"Your baby has no head."* That sentence razors through my psyche again and again. That is what the ultrasound technician said, on that fateful day. *"Your baby has no head."* I duck my whole body under the bubbles, holding my breath for what feels like eternity.

Your baby has no head.
Your baby has no head.
Your baby has no head.
Your baby has no head.
Your baby has no head.
Your baby has no head.
Your baby has no head.
Your baby has no head.
Your baby has no head.
Your baby has no head.
Your baby has no head.
Your baby has no head.
Your baby has no head.

How could a mother ever forget such a sentence? Instantly, Colin was relegated to a glob in my stomach. He was decreed a non-entity. With that sentence and in that instant, I didn't mourn a baby. Instead, I wondered what creature was in my uterus. Colin was immediately medically classified as a blob that was to be expelled, not a baby I was going to lose.

A baby needs a head.

A mother needs a head to mourn.

When I held him on the bed, he had a little cap on to cover up any skull deformities because of the neural tube defect. I saw his face and forehead, but I know sometimes the back of the head can be completely vacant, so most people don't want to see this. People want to remember their children as whole and pure and perfect. But Colin wasn't completely whole. Or maybe he was. I'll never, ever know because I didn't look at his skull. I could ask Orrie. I think he saw. Would he get angry with me if I asked? *"Stop dwelling on the past, Avril. There's no need for you to ask me about that. You have to start looking towards the future. Why keep bringing up the pain?"*

How could I be such a coward? What was I thinking? I don't even think I saw his bum. How strange that a mother has no idea what her son's bottom looks like? I try to fight through the fog to get glimpses of his behind, of the backs of his legs, of his knees. I can remember his knees. I can remember the entire front of him in pretty vivid detail, but I can't see anything from behind. Did I not turn him over to examine every single part of him before he was lost to me forever? How could I be so lazy?

I'm such a fool.

Then again, I wanted to hold him, not examine him. He wasn't a laboratory experiment that needed to be checked off and balanced. He was my baby, and I only had a limited time to experience him on this plane. No – this isn't something I get to beat myself up over. I didn't see the back of his head, but he saw my heart. That's better.

Am I getting better?
God? Am I getting better?

And for the first time in a long time, I think I hear an answer.

CHAPTER 33

I took twenty-one pictures of a butterfly today. I noticed it gracefully floating around the sandbox when I took Duet to the park. It was bright yellow with the most beautiful blue markings I've ever seen. Duet was in no mood to move from her play station, so I couldn't just wander off chasing the butterfly. I needed to be responsible and ensure my child wasn't accosted by a predator or get sand kicked in her face by other kids. So I just passively watched the butterfly gently float away in the wind currents, using its wings whenever the moment seemed right. The butterfly reminded me of Duet just zenning out wherever she is. I'm jealous of both of them.

So imagine my surprise when I come home to find the exact same butterfly just outside my kitchen window. I almost yelp. Duet senses my excitement. "What is it, Mommy? Who's out there?"

"It's a butterfly, sweetie. You stay there while I take some pictures." Duet places her nose on the glass, leaving little smudge marks of grease that she creatively uses as finger paint on the window. I'm grateful the butterfly doesn't pay any attention and stays on the outside pane. "Did you want to come outside with me, Du? Do you want to help me take photos?" I realize my mistake as soon as I vocalize it. If I really want to be productive, I can't have Duet interacting with the camera. Thankfully, she's too interested in creating steam on the window with her breath. "Can I stay here, Mommy? Am I old enough now?"

"Sure, sweetie. I'll be right outside."

I slip out to the front yard, clicking away. I'm not sure what I will do with all the images, but I'm too caught up in the activity to care. Then it hits me that I left Duet all alone in the house for the first time ever...

...and everything was okay.

She is now old enough to be by herself for little stints. These tiny stretches will become longer and longer. Eventually, my daughter will move away from home, never to need oversight again. I wait for the melancholy to sink in, but for some strange reason I find it more comforting than anything else. Life goes on. And keeps going on. This is something to celebrate instead of fearing.

I look at Duet in the kitchen window. She's still intently drawing smiley faces on the glass. I wave at her, then shake like a puppy waking up from a nap. Duet is growing up, but so am I. I look around for the butterfly but it's off to its next adventure. I look back at Duet in the window, getting more independent while being happy the entire time. A spring of joy squeaks through my chest, just under the ribcage. It spreads out through my shoulder blades, pulsating under my neck. I don't want to ruin the feeling, so I just whisper a prayer of thanks to God for creating powerful creatures like butterflies.

I remember once when Joanie and I were little, we were lying on our lawn, aimlessly crafting characters out of the marshmallow clouds in the sky. Our property had a patch of grass on a slope that made the absolute best place to relax. The grass was longer and greener, making it deliciously sweet to chew while we lay on our backs and contemplated life. Eventually, Mom came by to check up on us. After some gentle prodding, she settled herself between us to share perspectives of what the clouds looked like or what the birds were thinking as they swooped overhead. The sun was the perfect temperature that day. I remember feeling like a breeze was blowing from ear to ear across us like it was stringing beads, joining the three of us together. A butterfly flew by, so very close that it felt like it was going to tickle our cheeks and noses. My mom told us to never underestimate butterflies. They look delicate and weak, but they have gone through changes and pain we can't even fathom.

"To look pretty?" Joanie asked.

"No," Mom replied. "To fly."

CHAPTER 34

Duet's gone to bed for the night so I decide to zoom around the Internet, looking up more information about anencephaly. Orrie is at work, which makes it a good time to explore. I try to do my searching when Orrie isn't around because I don't want him to think I'm obsessing about Colin (because I'm not). It's been eighteen weeks now and that means over four months have gone by since Colin died. Even though it sounds like such a short time, it's actually been an eternity. It's officially been long enough to regenerate the red blood cells in my body. All the blood in my body that I didn't lose hemorrhaging after Colin's birth has been renewed. I'm a completely different person than I was almost four months ago. I might share some of the same personality traits, but my internal organs and mental geography have been so mutated that I've actually come out of this a transformed Avril. I know others recognize this because everyone looks at me strangely. Or maybe they look that way because they still don't know how to look at me.

While on my secret surf, I come across a couple of people who have blogs dealing with their babies dying. Initially,

I shrink back from the screen's words and images. But then I lean in because my perspective changes. I see the sites as another constructive way of actualizing the misery, so eventually it can all go away. Bandages don't just hide the cut; they let you know there's something there that needs protecting. The hope is that eventually the bandage will be taken off to reveal a healed body.

Even though a child dying is all too real, in some ways it doesn't feel real at all. You begin to see everything outside of yourself, like it's happening to another person. Obviously, something this tragic couldn't be happening to you, so either you must be dreaming, or you're watching a really depressing movie you've gotten too engrossed in. Better switch the channel before you lose your mind. But the remote control doesn't work, and the TV won't turn off. You're trapped in a reality program from Kafka that never seems to end. Your heart keeps beating, you keep breathing. People around you keep living, expecting you to join in. But it still never seems to be real. Even after it happens, sometimes it doesn't feel like a memory as much as a remembrance of another person's experience. There's no way you could imagine dealing with the pain of losing a child. Other people are strong enough, but not you. Not that it matters, because it will never happen to you. Things like that happen to other people.

Best not to think about it.

I'm deeply thinking about not thinking about it when I get busted by Orrie. He quietly walks in the room, ruffles my hair and asks what I'm doing. I feel like I've been caught looking at porn or something. I shift in my chair, trying to block his view of the screen. "Nothing," I pant. "I'm just checking my mail."

"But you're on a couple of sites, too." He bends closer. "What are you looking at?"

"Is this the Spanish Inquisition? Can't I just go on the computer?" I nervously banter, wondering how I can covertly close the sites. I can't think of any possible way except kicking the plug out of the socket, and I'm not graceful enough for that maneuver.

Orrie takes off his sweater. "Sure, just wondering."

"I'm not looking at anything."

"Okay."

"Why do you care?"

"Just asking," Orrie responds, honestly enough.

"Actually, I'm looking at a person's homepage," I test him. "She had a little boy who died of anencephaly. She has a blog here talking about it and stuff."

"Shouldn't you be doing something else? It's nice outside this evening. How about I make us a cocktail and we sit outside?"

"Do you want to look at it with me?" I ask.

"No, I feel like going out on the deck. Do you want to join me? It would be fun."

"No," I sigh.

"How about we check the sites another time?" Orrie asks. "Just not right now, okay? I don't want to yet."

I smile. "Sounds good. Just let me know."

"I will."

I slowly drag the mouse across the table, closing the pages. "Hey, Orrie?"

"Yeah?"

"You're right - it is a nice night. It's a good idea to hang out on the deck for a bit."

Orrie smiles at me as he heads towards the kitchen. I get ready to follow him, pulling myself away from the screen. We used to hang out on the deck all the time. It will be nice to return to the normalcy of the evening, like meeting up with an old friend after a winter break. I go outside and gaze at the stars. There's one shining really brightly towards the left of the horizon.

"You'll be my Colin Star," I whisper to the heavens. "And all of us will be together tonight." I wait for a bit to ascertain if this is comforting or creepy. Is this moving forward or is this a step back in my healing journey? Is it okay to do this?

Orrie comes through the door and gives me a hug. We sit on the wooden chairs, looking up at the sky. Does he see the same star? Did he give it a name, too? I want to ask him, but stop myself because I'm enjoying the moment. I don't want to ruin it by infusing something wrong into the occasion. Instead, I pull closer to the propane heater that Orrie started to cut the chill of the evening. I drink my cocktail, tracing the condensation forming on the cold glass. We talk about our days, what we're doing with our tomorrows, and what we should plan for the upcoming weekend. Neither of us mentions anything important, because we're both terrified to break this moment. It's so incredibly necessary to have lovely, normal moments like these.

CHAPTER 35

I'm freaking out here.

There's literally a newborn at every corner in this mall.

I can't breathe.

I'm sweating.

I saw a newborn yesterday at the grocery store. I asked the mom if I could take a peek at him and she, of course, said yes. The more admirers the better. I looked in, making eye contact with his huge blue eyes. I quickly thanked the mother, then rushed on. I felt I had accomplished something. I was able to look at a baby who lived longer than Colin did, and I survived the vision. My eyes didn't burn out of my head, and I didn't burst into flames. I was proud of myself.

Today I'm freaking out. Is this some sort of post-traumatic stress from yesterday's peek? I think my heart is going to explode from underneath my ribs at any moment. How exciting would that be to the other shoppers if I died here in front of the handbag store? I recognize no one cares or is paying attention, but I feel like there's a gaping hole beside me where a baby should be. I feel like I'm in a moving picture and someone has stuck a shadow through the print. No matter where I move, the black wall behind the frame is beside me. I don't even feel like I'm in a color photo anymore.

Is this the beginning of a panic attack? Am I going to have panic attacks every time I see a baby? Would I still be freaking out if Duet were here? I left Duet with Gloria so I could go shopping. Am I that incomplete that I can't be alone anymore? I decide to embrace the horror, taking a detour to a children's clothing store to search for some items for Duet. I'll show the other shoppers that even though my daughter isn't with me right now, I still have a child to shop for. I'm a mother. I'm not here just shopping for myself or my cat.

I click, click, click through the clothes and decide there's nothing here that interests me. Everything is either too expensive or too similar to what is already at home. I wander to the back of the store where they have items for babies 0-2 months old. It can't hurt to take a peek. It's not like I'm shopping, I'm just passing time between errands. There might be showers coming up and I should be prepared for them. Besides, I have to face my fears. I have to be around babies. I can't be scared of them forever. I'm busy convincing myself everything's cool when I see a neighbor's head over the clothes rack. I look down really quickly, like doing so is going to keep her from seeing me. There's a bit of the ostrich in every human.

"Avril?" She swoops in.

"Oh, hello, Lucy. How are you?"

"I'm fine, dear. How are you?" I can tell she's dying to ask me what I'm doing here.

"I'm fine. Fine, fine." I need to think up a reason for being here. I make up a pregnant friend. "Have you heard June's expecting?"

"June who?"

Think, think, think. "June Livingstone."

"Who's she?"

"Oh, I thought you knew her. I thought everyone knew her." I can hear a little panic in my voice. *I'm talking too fast.* "She's a very outgoing person who a lot of people seem to know. Oh well. She's expecting in another month or so. I just figured I'd pick up something for her shower. I guess the world is bigger than you think, because I honestly thought you knew June." *Shut up, shut up, shut up.* "She's lovely – a great friend. She seems to be everyone's friend. It's too bad you don't know her. I think she's going to get a lot of presents at her baby shower." I bite my lip to stop myself from saying anything more.

"So how have you been lately?" She tilts her head and draws her eyebrows together, her lower lip jutting out.

"I'm great."

"Under the circumstances," she coos. She pats my arm and I sharply pull it away. I grab a pair of red overalls hanging on the rack beside me to cover my rudeness.

"Yes. Yeah, I'm great under the circumstances."

"There are a lot of little babies here today. It must be hard." Her cat eyes drill at me.

"No, I'm okay. It's been a couple of months now. I've been dealing with things really well. There's Orrie and Duet to keep me going. We've all been doing really well."

"That's good, dear." She points at the overalls. "So is that what you're going to buy?"

"Yeah, I think red's a good choice. That way it can be suitable for either a girl or a boy."

"You were going to have a little boy, weren't you?"

"Yes, I did ... I ... I did have a little boy. His name was Colin," I stammer.

"Sorry, that's what I meant." She's not sorry at all.

I uncomfortably look around the store. "Well, I better get going. I have a lot of errands to run." I take the outfit with me to cover up my lie. It's only twenty bucks, I can afford it.

She flashes a big grin. "See you later, dear."

"I imagine you will," I say as I turn to leave.

She looks at me strangely. I shrug my shoulders as if I'm quite sure of what I meant by that. I feel her eyes boring into my back as I go down the aisle, so I duck behind a clearance rack of toddler snowsuits to insulate my body from her gaze and wait there until it is safe to leave.

CHAPTER 36

Orrie is late again tonight. I think I've been stirring my herbal tea for around ten hours or so. I keep hoping the chamomile will perform its magic, but I'm experienced enough to know it really won't work. I'm going to be awake for hours sipping tea and looking at the clock. I'm actually thankful for a mosquito buzzing around my head. Hunting it down will be a welcome distraction.

God, I feel so alone. I automatically look up towards the ceiling as I think this. I am Godless and alone. Wow, it feels so scary to voice that. Do I really believe it? *Why hast thou forsaken me, God?* Am I reaching a cresting point where I could tip towards losing my relationship with God? The possibility is terrifying.

Does it scare me because it makes me feel more alone

or

does it scare me because I fear retribution

or

does it scare me because if I truly don't believe in God anymore, do I really want to exist?

I definitely need God more than he needs me. I think I can live with being hurt and confused about God not caring about me, but I don't know if I can survive without any God at all. Is this why I believe in him? Is it a survival mechanism? What do I get out of God? What does God do for me? I constantly fear him. Even having these thoughts makes me a bit frightened that I'll get cancer or some other punishment. *So what did I do to deserve Colin dying, God? What horrible act did I think or do? Why punish me while you let others get away with dirty deeds?*

Suddenly, I sit up and take notice of the mosquito trying to get inside my ear. I swat at it and spend ten minutes or so trying to catch it. Finally, I squish it against the wall in the hallway. I look at the gore I created on the white paint, wondering whose blood is intermingled with the mosquito's messy remains. I'm about to clean it, but then leave it as a victory smear.

I check on Duet again to pass the time. She has a nasty habit of putting the quilt over her head lately, and I've become compulsive about peeking in her room to make sure she's breathing. I don't mind waking her up to move the covers. It's almost a bonus if she stirs because then I have an excuse to slip in her bed and cuddle her back to sleep. I continuously vow to stop creeping in the next night, but the cycle seems to continue.

I hear the garage door open so I rush downstairs to welcome Orrie home. He comes in, looking haggard. Even his briefcase has seen better days. I ask him if he would like a tea. He does, so I pick out his favourite blend and heat up the kettle.

"Hard day?"

"No, it was pretty good." He turns his head so I can't see his jawline. "You?"

"Fine, I guess. Gloria was asking if we had an end date set for her. I told her that we'd like to extend it for at least another couple of months. Does that sound okay with you?"

"Sure, makes sense. She's great, plus Duet loves her."

The kettle starts whistling so I prepare Orrie's brew. I bring his cup over to the table. He holds it by the handle, blowing on it before he gingerly sips the hot contents.

"Thanks, Avie." He kisses me on the forehead in appreciation.

"No problem, pleased to do it."

Orrie looks at me as he takes another sip. "Are you sure you're okay? You look a bit down."

"I've just been thinking, I guess."

"Yeah, about what?"

"God."

"Oh," Orrie laughs in spite of himself. "Is that all?"

I smirk at him. "Well, you asked."

"And what are you thinking?"

"I don't know. A bunch of things, like - Colin's death was blameless. What do mothers do when their children are murdered? What do they do when their children are raped? How can they still believe in a God after that? Or do they need to believe in him even more because they've come eye-to-eye with the red glow of the Devil? And if the Devil exists, is that proof enough that God's around, as well?"

Orrie closes his eyes, slowly massaging his temples. "So are you saying that you believe in God because you believe in the Devil?"

"No. Well, maybe. Bugs are from the devil. No one ever has nice thoughts when a fly lands on their arm or buzzes around their head. But God created flies and mosquitoes. Why did God create evil?"

"I would say that God created evil so we could have a choice. He loves us enough to give us the free choice to deny him. He loves us enough that he doesn't want us to love him in a robotic fashion. If we want to adore him, he rejoices."

"Yeah, but that doesn't look as black and white to me now. Nothing does. That's why I can't sleep at night. Grey doesn't even cut it anymore. Life is ripping me to shreds with its shades of psychedelic purple."

Orrie comes over, giving me a big hug. "Avie, I get it. I'm hurting too. But we can't stop believing in God because he doesn't address our every whim. He's not our personal genie. He doesn't ceaselessly serve us."

I shake free. "Your confidence is annoying." Orrie lets me go, but he looks so sad that I circle my arms completely around his waist. "Sorry, I don't mean that. I'm still a bit raw. I know I believe in God, but I'm just not sure how much I trust him right now. Is that okay?"

"Of course it is," Orrie soothes as he kisses the top of my head. Just hearing this assurance makes my soul feel like it is being massaged with a menthol salve.

Orrie gives me a quick squeeze. "Are you ready for bed now?"

"Yes," I yawn. "I'm totally exhausted. Let's go."

CHAPTER 37

Duet and I are playing with pink horsies. I'm the magical being who comes from above to tell her all of the creatures are allowed flight. As I impose this magical free rein, I tell Duet I have to go to the bathroom, because even magical mommies have to go sometimes. This is cool, and for three minutes, all is right in our world.

And then I go to the bathroom.

And I pee.

And for the first time since I was pregnant with Colin, I have my period.

"Gloria?" I yelp from the washroom. "Gloria, can you hear me?"

"Yes, Avril, I'm downstairs. Just a second." I hear her voice get louder as she comes closer.

"Where are you?"

"I'm in the bathroom. Gloria, could you do me a favor? Can you take Duet to the ice cream store to pick out a cone? I know it's outside of your responsibilities, but if you don't mind, I would really appreciate it."

Gloria gently knocks on the door. "Are you okay?" she asks, nervously.

"Oh, yes," I squawk from the toilet. "I'm good, good. I'm just having a really difficult bowel movement. I need some time to myself." I seriously can't believe I just said that. I honestly can't believe this is the best excuse I can come up with under pressure.

"Okay … we'll be back in about a half-hour. Is there something you'd like me to pick up at the drug store while I'm out?"

"No, I'll be great once this passes." I obviously don't mean that the way it comes out, but I'm neither smart nor articulate enough to make a verbal recovery, so I just awkwardly leave it be.

I hear Gloria talking to Duet. It's a bit muffled because she's trying to be quiet, plus they're down the hallway. "Let's go for a walk, sweetie," she encourages.

I hear a soft thud. "I'm playing with Mommy now."

"Your mom needs a little time in the bathroom. She'll play with you again when we get back." Gloria's voice becomes more muffled, but I think I hear her say the word "poop". That's all it takes to put Duet in a fantastic mood again. I hear her giggle as they bang around, presumably putting on their shoes and coats.

The front door slams shut, leaving me alone on the toilet, bleeding into the porcelain basin in an ever so normal fashion. I didn't really think before calling Gloria, so I don't really know why I'm here alone. Why did I need to be alone? What am I going to do now that I'm alone? Am I going to cry? Am I going to freak out? Why do I need the assurance of solitude?

I have no answers. As my blood makes the toilet water redder and redder, I try to come up with a logical conclusion. *Okay, think – what do I need to think?* As I'm thinking, I realize I don't have any tampons or pads. I'm totally unprepared. On every level. I mean, I consciously knew this was going to happen again. It's natural. My body is naturally doing what it's naturally supposed to be doing. So – naturally – I should have been prepared for this entirely natural event to take place.

Naturally.

Maybe if I wait long enough, I won't have to do anything about it. Maybe if I stay here for four to six days, everything will sort itself out.

Why have I put off buying tampons? Was I afraid of what that would mean? That it would mean my body is now physically prepared to have another baby? That my body is totally out of sync with my brain? How can my body be ready so soon? Why isn't it grieving? Why doesn't it care? *Okay, time's up, Avril. Let's get going. Clock is ticking. Come on – enough already. Let's move on now. Must gush ahead.*

How can my body be so callous and unfeeling?

Doesn't it know it's not natural to move on so quickly?

CHAPTER 38

I have been connected to my friend, Emma, since birth. Our mothers were friends and we've been having play dates since we were babies.

"So, I guess you've heard?" I ask Emma over the phone.

It's really strange yet comforting that when you're true friends with someone, it doesn't matter how long you've been apart. You quickly get back into the zone. I consider Emma to be one of my best friends, even though I rarely talk to her anymore. She met an Englishman in university, and they moved to London to live close to his family after they graduated. Physical distance has kept us apart, but the emotional bond will eternally be strong. We have too much history to be anything else but mates. We failed swimming lessons together because we couldn't stop giggling during the mouth-to-mouth resuscitation trials. It was too close to kissing your sister to be anything else but really weird.

"Yeah, my mother told me. I've wanted to call for the longest time, but there never seemed to be an opportunity," Emma apologizes. "Plus the time difference. I'm really sorry it's taken this long to connect." I can hear her sorrow through the telephone line.

I got drunk for the first time with Emma. Her father was an alcoholic and wasn't concerned with keeping vodka out of his teenage daughter's reach. There was enough to go around, I guess. I don't know how much we had, but it was enough to keep me away from the stuff for a long, long time. I think I lost around ten pounds after the event because I couldn't keep food down for about a week or so. We snuck away to her tree fort and went shot for shot. Her parents and my mom thought we were staying at the other's house for the night, so we were safe from getting caught. We were supposed to meet up with some other friends in town, but after about an hour of playing century, we couldn't get down the ladder. Fortunately, we weren't drunk enough to think we could jump out of the fort. We stayed all night up in the tree, slurring to each other until the wee hours.

"Yeah, it's been a tough year." I sigh into the phone receiver. "Lots of growing up."

After we graduated high school, Emma and I separated, enrolled in different universities. We had applied to the same schools, but she got a scholarship to our number one choice, and I didn't. She was such a good friend that I wasn't even jealous. I was content to escape my small town with its smaller ideas, plus I was still able to move a plane ride away from my birthplace.

Emma's dad died second year of university. He had a massive heart attack while he was mowing the lawn. At the funeral, everyone talked about how mowing your lawn and shoveling snow were the two big killers. Apparently, if one didn't get you the other one will. No one mentioned the alcoholism. I flew home for the funeral. I wasn't flush with cash, or anything, but her dad was someone I had grown up with and feared my whole life. I almost felt if I didn't come home for the event, he would haunt me from the afterlife.

Emma seemed fine throughout the wake and funeral. She didn't cry, or anything. Her mom seemed almost relieved sitting beside the casket. I had to stop myself from telling her how good she looked. The compliment didn't seem appropriate under the circumstances. Emma just appeared bored. I remember thinking that she didn't fit my description of what a grieving daughter should look like. Isn't she supposed to be devastated? Shouldn't she be flipping out? Aren't there supposed to be tears? I felt disappointed in her; it was like she didn't even care. Neither one of them did.

The day after her father's funeral, we got together for coffee at my mom's house. I told her that she seemed to be doing well. She told me she was still in shock. She said it was like a part of her body was missing. He was too strong to be anything else but here. It's like a mountain that you see every day is all of a sudden gone without any explosion. I asked her if she was sad. I didn't know why I asked such an inane question. Fortunately, ignorance is forgivable amongst friends.

She told me that of course she was sad her dad died. She just didn't know how she was supposed to deal with something this big. Things like this don't happen in real life. I never quite knew what she meant until Colin's death. People's emotions aren't fictional representations you see on a movie screen. Real life is more tragic and less cinematic.

Emma takes a sharp breath in. "Oh my gosh, Avril, I'm so sorry. I have to go. Benny just jumped on the table. I have to get him. I'll call you back."

I say goodbye to the dial tone, hoping her son gets off the furniture with no scrapes or bruises. I go about my business, without any tears, without any drama, and without any theatrical glory. Life's just like that. And that's not a bad thing. It's just that life doesn't have a cool soundtrack, and it wouldn't make a great movie most of the time.

I've been having a number of interactions with school friends lately. Carol, a neighbor who lived down the street when we were kids, popped in for a visit last week. Carol moved away with her mother after her parents divorced in grade seven. She comes back home periodically to visit her father, Joanie and me. Usually it's great to reconnect. This time it wasn't because I really didn't want her to catch up on my life. I wanted to be the person she remembers from before. I wanted to be the carefree one without any major problems in her life, even if I never really had that life to begin with.

I was really tempted to lie to her, to tell her nothing has happened lately. *Things have been rather uninteresting, overall. And you?* It would just be so nice not to bring it all up again. Death really never ends. It sounds so final, until you realize it's only truly concluded for the one who died. Everyone else has to go on reliving and retelling the tale of the death over and over and over again.

The only thing that kept me from lying is my fear of being caught. I knew she'd be seeing other people who would bring it up, and then they'd all be gossiping about how strange it was if I never mentioned the fact my baby died. I'm almost at the point of not caring how abnormal it would be to hide it from people who don't know. I'm sick of being strong enough to deal with it on a continual basis. It's like being on a roller coaster that makes my eyes hurt each time I get to the top of the track. It's always so fresh to the people I tell. They haven't dealt with it before, so the story is newly tragic and raw. I almost have to force myself to tell the story with more emotion, instead of a robotic play-by-play, like reading a yellowed telegram.

Yes, my son died. Stop.

He was three hours old. Stop.

I wasn't there because I was being operated on. Stop.

He died in Orrie's arms. Stop.

I almost died. Stop.

Stop.

Stop.

Stop.

Sometimes people cry when I tell them. I've been living with this long enough that I almost look at them like I'm analyzing a patient through a window. It's not new to me anymore. Nothing is as sore and exposed anymore. My emotional pus is now a scar. Would I feel such sorrow for someone else? Who am I to deserve acquaintances that care so much?

Joanie thinks I have to start allowing myself to feel things again. She believes I've become too detached. I tell her if she doesn't stop bothering me, I'm going to detach myself from her for good. I love my sister, but I'm sick of being psychoanalyzed by her. I know she means well, but I have a sneaking suspicion she stays awake at nights wondering about me and deciphering my moves. It's a bit creepy and pathetic. Joanie wants everyone to believe she has everything going for her. She's the exciting one with the career, the cars and the friends. I'm the mouse who stays home with her daughter and doesn't go out to play with adults very often. I sometimes think it drives her crazy that I'm a happier person than she is, even after all I've been through. She has it together, so she should be the one who administers advice. I should be turning to her more often but I don't, and it annoys her to no end. I'm sure she's quizzing Carol, going through the play-by-play of our conversation. *"So did she cry? Did she seem upset? She's keeping it all in, you know. It's not healthy. More wine?"*

CHAPTER 39

"Why do you have to disagree with me all the time, Avril? Why can't you just accept I know what I'm talking about?"

"Because sometimes you're not right."

"If I'm not sure of what I'm saying, then I don't say it."

"Well, you seem to talk quite a bit."

I look over at Orrie while he splits his time between our argument and playing his silly video game. He's always right. Always. If he said wood was made of plastic, you'd be an idiot to disagree with him because he always, always knows what he's talking about.

"We need to talk about what's wrong with you lately. It's like you have a chip on your shoulder all the time," he bites.

I glare at him. "There's nothing wrong with my shoulder."

He looks up from the screen. "Then what's going on?"

"What do you think is wrong? Look, let's just drop it. You were right. You're always right, Orrie. I shouldn't have corrected you." I turn to leave the room.

"Stop that. Stop being so passive-aggressive with me."

"Sorry, you're right. I should stop." Jerk.

"How about we discuss this like rational beings?" Orrie continues.

I trounce back to the living room. "I don't want to talk about it. I need to get milk. I'll be back in ten minutes." I grab my keys from the bowl on the table. "Actually, I told Joanie I would pop by. I'm going over there for a bit." I yank open the door and stomp to the car.

After approximately twenty minutes of complaining to Joanie about Orrie, I finally get to the heart of the matter. "I find myself being irrationally bitter with him sometimes," I confess. "It's not that I necessarily blame Orrie for what happened with Colin, but I can't help thinking if I had never met him, none of this would have happened."

"You can't blame Orrie for this, Avril. You can't blame anyone. That's why you're so upset." Joanie pulls a tissue from the box on her coffee table and hands it to me.

I dab at my eyes, then blow my nose. "Am I so dissatisfied with my life that I wish I could give up my years with him? I used to think regret was one of the worst experiences in life; that it's better to do something than to regret never having done it. When was I ever that naive?"

"I don't know what to say, sweetie. If you never met Orrie, you wouldn't have Duet, either."

"I know. I feel guilty even thinking this." I stuff the tissue into my pocket.

"You're not thinking it, you're exploring thoughts. That's different."

"I just feel so useless now. My life doesn't have the meaning it used to. If I never married Orrie, would things be different? Would I have five children and a career on the side? Would I have started up my own company? Would I be living in Argentina? Would I be rich? Who would I be?"

"You'd be the same person, but you'd have different experiences. That's all."

"What's Jonah been up to lately?" I ask out of the blue. Joanie looks at me like she has no clue who I'm talking about. "You know – Jonah. That guy we met on the school trip."

Joanie thinks for a minute, then widens her eyes. "You mean the guy you had a crush on?"

"Yeah."

Joanie throws her head back, laughing. "You mean the guy who caught you kissing that other guy?"

"Um, yeah." I had conveniently forgotten about that part.

"Why did you ever kiss that guy, anyway? You didn't even like him."

"I was funneling beer."

"That was dumb." Joanie gets up from her chair.

"Noted."

"I don't think Jonah lives around here. I haven't seen him in years."

"He probably lives in Manhattan with a glorious apartment, four kids and a beautiful wife," I sigh as I sink into the massive couch.

"Who knows," Joanie distantly chirps from the kitchen.

I wonder if anyone wonders about Orrie. If so, I wonder if they are really glad they never hooked up with him because of the mess his life is in. Or is Orrie's life in a mess? Is he happy? He works in a pretty impressive law firm and isn't hard to look at, even in the mornings. He hasn't gained the extra pudge that has afflicted my mid-section, and he gets along with other people. All in all, he's probably an appealingly decent package.

I wonder if anyone wonders about me. Is there anyone out there who thinks about who I used to be, and what I used to look like? Does anyone wish his pillow was beside mine? I wonder if I'm worthy of any wonderings. I wonder if anyone's wonderings would turn into nightmares if they realized what it would mean to be by my side.

I wonder if Orrie wonders about someone else, because my pillow is really cold lately.

CHAPTER 40

I haven't been to a doctor's office since my six-week post check-up. Now that I'm here, I'm not even weirded out about it. I thought I would be all fidgety and sweaty, but I'm just as bored as I used to be when I had to wait for any examination. Maybe I'm dealing so well because the appointment isn't actually for me. I'm at our family doctor's with Duet for her annual checkup. My last appointment was with my OB-GYN, so this is the first time I've seen Dr. Belcher since Colin died. I don't even know if he knows about what happened. Is he going to ask me how I am and when I say fine, he'll believe me without question? How will I reply to his asking if anything out of the ordinary has been going on with my body? Or will he not ask me any questions about myself, sticking to queries about Duet?

Now I'm getting sweaty.

Crap.

The waiting room is full of people with dull eyes and old magazines from summers past. I think I see a spider's web in the corner of the ceiling, but it's just a shadow playing tricks on me. The air feels heavy and moist. Either there's no air conditioning in the building or they're conserving energy. It feels rife with germs.

I look at the various mouths of the people waiting alongside me and envision them exhaling their diseases into the air. No one looks really sick, though. Why are they here if they're not sick? Maybe some of them have walking pneumonia. I had a friend who had that. He didn't go to the hospital until his girlfriend forced him to. He was sweating the sheets wet at night because he was so hot. He said his girlfriend was more grossed out than concerned for his health, but he was grateful she put her foot down and made him get medical attention, just the same. His doctor said if he had waited another week, he'd be dead.

"Excuse me."

I look up at an old man staring down at me. "Sorry?"

"I just have to get past you." He looks at me, then the coffee table.

"Oh, just a sec." I shove my chair back a little.

The old man grunts as he sits down. "It's busy today, huh?"

"Yeah, must be that time of year." I hate saying things that don't really make sense, but it just slips out of me. I can't see the old man calling me on it. I'm just making polite conversation. I don't have to be engaging or interesting. It doesn't matter that it's the middle of summer and there's nothing on the go. It doesn't matter that I just said something stupid.

"Yep. Usually it's the winter, but now it's the summer," the old man replies.

Looks like I'm not the only master of trite expressions. I decide I like my old friend. We're on the same wavelength.

He twitches his head in Duet's direction. "That your rascal over there?"

Usually I don't like it when people refer to my little girl in such terms. Typically it brings out the snob in me, but for some reason it seems natural and pure when he says it, so I let it go without any bad vibes. "Yep, she's mine."

He scrunches his one eyebrow, looking at me through the long hairs. "So, who's your people?"

"Pardon?"

"Who's your people? Where are you from?"

"Ah. I'm from town. We live on Elm Street."

"Who's your people, though? Your grandparents, father? Are they from here?"

"Yeah, my parents used to live on Pine Street. My mother still lives there. My dad was Harold Lewis. Well, he still is Harold Lewis, but he doesn't live on Pine Street anymore. Mom's name is Bertha. People call her Bertie."

"Oh, so you're the girl who had the dead baby."

Smack.

I don't think I've ever been winded by a sentence before. I stare at the old man, opening and closing my mouth like a fish. I glance around the room, but everyone still looks as bored as ever. I don't think anyone else hears the zinging in their ears. The world hasn't stopped for anyone else. The old man innocently waits for my response like he asked me if it was raining outside.

"Ah, yeah, I guess so."

He nods his head. "Yeah, that's a shame."

I deeply inhale all the germs from the room and nod back.

"Sarah lost a baby sixty years ago. You never get over it. Owen. His name was Owen."

"Is Sarah your wife?"

"She was. She's in the Protestant cemetery on Caledonia Street. You can see her grave from the road when

181

you go by. It's in around four rows." He does a visual calculation and nods his head. "Yep, it's four rows."

"That's too bad," I lament, immediately regretting it. I hope he knows I'm referring to Sarah's death, and not where's she's placed in the cemetery. He just nods, so I know that he either knows what I was talking about, or doesn't care.

"So where's your baby?" he asks.

"Duet?"

"Is that its name?"

"Duet is my daughter." I point towards the toy box. "She's right there playing."

"No, your baby. Where's your baby buried?"

"Oh, we didn't bury him." I shift in my chair. "We cremated him." I honestly can't believe I'm talking about this with a complete stranger. It's too surreal. Up until now it's been such a personal event that only my friends, family and I have talked about. I breathe a little more quickly, and consciously have to stop before I get dizzy.

"Yeah, that's what people do nowadays. It's like the war."

"Pardon me?" I ask, exhaling really slowly. Slowly, slower, slow.

"It's like the war. There are a lot of bodies that never made it back home to the cemetery."

I nod. I have no idea what he's talking about, but I don't feel like asking about the connection. It's not that I don't care to know, it's just that I feel more comfortable in the dark.

"It's a long life," he continues. "Yep, there's a lot that goes on in life."

"Yep," I reply, thinking this is the best way to respond. For some reason, I don't want him to stop talking. I haven't had this deep and shallow of a conversation in a long time. I feel completely connected to this old man I don't know from a hole in the wall. I'm reveling in the uncomfortableness. It's like the feeling you get when you pick a scab or tweeze your eyebrows – it's sore, but it's an enjoyable pain that makes you continue the task. But this feels like I'm picking a scab while drinking a nice hot cup of cocoa.

"So, do you have any grandchildren?" I lean closer to him.

"I have seven grandkids. Four girls and four boys." I don't bother to tell him the miscalculation. I don't want to annoy him and halt the conversation.

A nurse appears in the doorway. "Mr. Stewart?"

"That's me," the old man mumbles as he slowly gets up from the chair. I bet he's in for arthritis or a hip replacement. I don't think he's ill. He's just in a lot of continuous pain. He doesn't say goodbye or even look back at me. I wish he was my grandfather or next-door neighbor so I could visit him to continue our talk over darkly steeped tea. But I know we'll never have tea. It would be too strange if I just popped into a stranger's house to say hello. He probably wouldn't even remember me, and besides, I only know where his wife resides in the cemetery.

Another nurse enters the room. "Duet Bale?"

Duet looks up from her play and makes eye contact with me. "It's time to go, Mommy."

I nod. "Let's go, Du."

"Who was that man you were talking to?" she asks.

I take her hand. "Just a man."

"What were you talking about?"

"Life."

"Whose life?"

"Ours," I realize in an off-handed, pointed way. "It's all of ours."

183

Duet lets go of my hand and streams down the hall, completely disinterested in keeping the inane conversation going. And for some inexplicable reason, I start humming as we go down the hall, past the ever-silent microbes, into the examining room where Dr. Belcher completes Duet's exam.

"Everything looks good," Dr. Belcher hangs the stethoscope back on its hook on the wall. "Her weight and height are good, her hearing and eyes look good. Everything is good."

"That's good," I say, not wanting to spoil the good, good trend.

"So, how are you?" he asks in a way that makes me think he knows about Colin.

"I'm good." I take a sudden interest in the contents of my purse, rummaging around for nothing, just wanting to avoid his potential look of pity.

"Are you sure? Would you like to talk about anything? Do you have any questions? I haven't seen you since ..." I now know he knows.

I force myself to look at him. "Yeah, I was going to the OB-GYN so I never bothered to have my annual checkup, or anything."

Dr. Belcher looks at my chart. "Sometimes things are outside of the medical realm. It's all part of a divine plan."

"Thinking things happen for a reason is egocentric," I sharply reply. "Things happen and we make a reason for it. That's the divine plan."

He coughs, shuffling his papers. "Yes, there's that." He moves his eyes away from mine and uncomfortably looks down at my chart again. "So have you had any problems since...?"

"His name was Colin." I lower my voice and check to see if Duet is listening to our conversation. She's happily playing with her toys and some medical supplies in the corner.

"Ah. That's a nice name. It's nice you named him."

"I had to for the death certificate."

"Oh," he looks down at his papers, yet again, for support. "Yes, that's right. I'm sorry."

"I'm good," I say again, even though it's not the right time to do so. I know I'm being viciously rude, but I can't help myself. Dr. Belcher isn't to blame for not being able to help me or Colin, but a sudden wave of visceral anger is rushing over me towards this man in a pink golf shirt hidden under his white scrubs. He has a tiny gold necklace with a pendant resting against his breastbone. Is he to blame? No. Do I savagely hate him at this moment?

Yes.

"Well, I guess I'll see you ..." He pauses, searching for the right thing to say. "I'll see you at your next annual, probably."

"That sounds good." I give him a fake smile.

"Good."

Good. Grand. Whatever.

On the way out of the office, I don't look back. I sense the doctor is still standing there wondering how he could have handled that better. Duet knows something is out of whack so she grabs my hand, leading me out of the waiting room. I foolishly look around for the old man to be sitting there, but of course he's gone back to his life and memories of his dead wife, son, and comrades.

I'm going to miss him.

He's the only one who gets me anymore.

CHAPTER 41

There are few things more tragic than something undone. Unfinished business. Is this what Colin is? Unfinished? How do other people think of Colin? I think of him as a baby who died, but do others recognize him this way? I wonder how many people have heard he was a miscarriage. I have no idea or control over what people are saying or thinking about him. Should I care if they have the correct details? Should I issue a press release? And why do I care? Why does this matter? Why is the distinction important?

I told people I didn't want a death announcement. Why didn't I want one? Was it because Orrie didn't want one, and I just agreed in my foggy haze? *Yes, Orrie. Whatever you say, Orrie. You know best, Orrie.* But I can't blame Orrie for taking responsibility in the face of unimaginable events. I can't blame him for being the one who was strong enough to make all of the decisions when I was walking around like a wet noodle. Ultimately, I can't blame Orrie for fulfilling my expressed wishes.

Then why am I angry with him most of the time? Sometimes, I look at Orrie and I want to slap him. Now that

I'm getting my legs back, I want to kick the man I married for being such an unfeeling beast. How could he have been so calm and businesslike? How could he have made all the arrangements – any arrangements – without breaking down more? Was he so strong because he didn't care?

"Can you pass the orange juice?" Orrie asks from across the table. He lifts his head from his newspaper and does a double take. "Why are you staring at me like that? What's up?"

I hand over the juice. "Why didn't you want a death announcement for Colin?"

"Why are you bringing that up now?" He pulls his eyebrows together and I can tell he's annoyed. "We already discussed this a long time ago. I'm on my way to work now."

"No, you're eating your breakfast."

"I'm eating my breakfast as part of the process of being on my way to work."

"Ah, I see." I pick a little piece from the corner of my toast and flick it onto my plate.

"Why are you bringing that up now?" he asks again.

"No reason, I was just thinking about something."

"What? What were you thinking about?"

I breathe out, slowly and methodically. "I don't know. Things. Lots of things."

He wipes his mouth with his napkin and gets up. "You shouldn't bemoan decisions that have already been made. We decided on the announcement a while ago. That should be that."

"I know. I was just thinking." I bite off a hangnail on my thumb and it starts to bleed.

"About what?"

"Nothing."

Orrie grabs his briefcase from the table and kisses Duet goodbye. "I'm going to work now." He distinctly doesn't bother to kiss me. I let it pass.

"Have a bath and relax a bit," he says as he picks cat hair off of his coat.

"But it's seven in the morning."

He looks up. "You know what I mean. Get Gloria to watch Duet, and have a nice soak. You can't obsess over things that are over and done with."

"Like Colin?"

"Who's Colin?" Duet chirps while squirting some of her cereal out of her mouth. She wasn't paying attention before, but now is fully engaged.

"No one, dear," Orrie answers.

"No one? How can you say that?" I throw what's left of my toast on my plate.

"Who's Colin?" Duet repeats.

"I have to go. You can sort this mess out yourself, Avril."

"Mess?" I yell. "Mess? How can you even say something like that? How can you refer to him as a mess?"

"Who's Colin? Colin, who's Colin? Why do you guys keep talking about him all the time?" Duet bangs her spoon on the cereal bowl, spilling milk all over the place.

I turn to her. "Duet, stop it."

"Look what you did." Orrie pulls open the door. "I have to go. We'll discuss this later."

I shoot up from my chair and storm after him into the garage. "After you're done with all your other, more important business, you mean."

"I don't need this first thing in the morning, Avril. I have a big day in front of me. I don't know what's wrong with you."

"My baby died. Your baby died. That's what's wrong."

"Who died? What baby?" Duet cries from inside the house.

Orrie pushes past me back into the house and kneels down beside Duet's chair, enveloping her in a hug. "No one, Du." Orrie soothes. "I'll see you when I get home. Love you." He looks at me after he gets up from holding Duet. "We'll talk about this later when you calm down."

"I'm calm now," I pout.

"I can't take you seriously when you're like this."

"Whatever." I reclaim my seat.

"It was your idea, Avril. You conveniently forget decisions that you yourself made. You conveniently forget that I was doing what you directed me to do." His tone is venomous. "You conveniently forget that I did what you wanted, while you didn't want to do anything at all."

"I'll see you later," I sheepishly mumble, knowing he's right. I can't think of anything else to say. I look over at Duet who is still dealing with an emotional overload, as well as a milk-covered shirt. I stand up and reach out my hand to her. "Come on, Du. Let's get you cleaned up."

"But I want to know who died." She crosses her little arms over her chest. "Did Colin die? Who's Colin? Is he the little boy from church?"

"What little boy?" I ask.

"The little boy they pray about at church."

"What church?"

"The one Daddy and I go to. You used to go there too."

I look at Orrie. "What is she talking about?"

"I took her to church with me a couple of times over the winter. It's no big deal."

"You did what?" I feel like I was cheated on. "Why didn't you tell me?"

"You needed time to yourself and I wanted to go. Even if you didn't feel like going to church, that doesn't mean I can't go. It's not all about you, Avril."

"Why are you fighting?" Duet pulls on my hand. "Who died? Why are you angry?"

Orrie walks out, slamming the door. I pick up Duet and head towards the bathroom to clean up the mess.

"Mommy, who's Colin?" Duet demands as she plays around in the bathtub.

I swish around some bubbles. "We don't need to talk about that, honey."

"But you wanted Daddy to talk about him. You wanted to talk about him before."

I get up from beside the tub to brush my teeth. "I don't want to now, sweetie."

"Why?"

I close my eyes. "Because I'm tired."

"Why?"

I spit out the toothpaste. "Because I don't sleep much lately."

"Why?"

Good question. "Because I stay up late."

"Why do you stay up late? You never let me do that. Do you stay up past your bed time?"

"Yep."

"Why?"

"Because I'm not tired at night."

"But you're tired now?"

I nod as I look at my reflection in the mirror. There are very dark circles under my eyes.

"Who's Colin?"

"Colin is a little baby we knew …" I trail off. I crouch back down beside the tub. "Wow, Duet. Look at those bubbles." I excitedly swirl the frothy water. I know I'll fail to change the subject unless I pull out the big guns. "Want to go for an ice cream after your bath?"

"Really?"

"Yes, we did such a great job cleaning you up that we deserve to get some ice cream when the shop opens."

"Does Colin like ice cream? Is he coming?"

"No, honey. Colin's not here."

"Where is he?"

"He's not here. Du – here's the thing. I'll get you two scoops of ice cream if we talk about something else."

"Why?"

"Because it's a contest. If you can talk about other things until we get the ice cream, you are going to get two scoops of any kind of ice cream you want."

"What?" She asks in disbelief. Such a glorious event has never happened to her before.

I look deeply into her eyes. "Any kind at all."

Duet waits for a second, knowing something is up, but doesn't want to punch the gift horse in the mouth. "Even though it's before lunch time?" she challenges.

"Yep, it's that big of a contest." I hold my breath, knowing I am a bad, bad mother.

"Okay. Let's start now," she yells with glee.

Oh well – being a bad mother does have its advantages when necessary. I can live with it. I'm just not going to share this particular parenting technique with Orrie. Just another family secret I'll keep in my pocket.

Later that night I walk around the house picking up Duet's toys that are chaotically scattered all over the place. Duet is sleeping and it's really quiet because Orrie isn't home. I don't have the television or radio on, but I can hear the humming of the appliances in the kitchen. It's not exactly white noise – more of an opaque sound – but it is background enough to make me feel contented and calm.

I pick up a teddy bear from Orrie's desk. Usually when I pick up toys or other pseudo baby items, I feel a sense of loss, but tonight I feel fine. I have no idea why. I don't want to think about it too much. I'm afraid if I figure out the puzzle, I will break it. I don't want to jeopardize this quiet, bliss-like sensation.

I think:

I have a little girl.

I have a little girl who is healthy and wholesome and pure and awesome.

I have a little girl who calls me mommy, and when she cries, I comfort her and she feels better.

I am a mom of a living child.

From habit, I search around my psyche for a bit of pain – there's still a part of me that doesn't feel right when I'm perfectly happy. I know if I roll it around my brain enough, I can find a tear in my soul somewhere, but tonight I stop short of the pulse point. I stop short, and I still feel fine. I have a lot to be thankful for, even though I have a lot to be so sad about. I need to start concentrating on the parts of my life that are working out – and there are quite a few. I have a perfect daughter I love more than words can describe. I have a husband who is an exceptional lifetime companion and puts up with me when he really, really shouldn't have to. I'm financially stable enough that I can stay home with Duet on a full-time basis, so I get to grow up with her, seeing all of her accomplishments and strides.

I have it all.

I just don't have Colin. And I can live with that. I will never forget him, or stop wanting him, but I can accept that he's not with me. I can accept it, and I can live with it, and I can keep going.

"Hey," Orrie whispers, breaking the silence.

"Hey. I never even heard you come in."

"I can tell. You're in a bit of a daze. Everything okay?"

"Yeah," I nod. I instinctively go to hug him hello, but then pull back. "It actually is. Or at least it's getting there."

Orrie takes my hand. "I'm sorry about this morning."

"That's okay. I'm sorry about a lot of things." I squeeze his hand in response.

"Do you want to talk about it?" Orrie asks.

"No, not really. Want to watch some late night talk shows instead?"

Orrie looks at me and really (really) smiles for the first time in a long time. "Yeah, that would be great. Just give me a minute to get ready for bed."

"Sounds wonderful," I smile. And I truly mean it.

CHAPTER 42

Each year, my neighborhood has a family fair that's constructed to bring the community together, to bond the family unit and to create favorable press releases about the benefits. Each year, we have kept away from said fair because Orrie is vehemently opposed to anything he deems a waste of money, or that involves crowds of people. Each year, he has found other important things to do to keep us from attending the fair. Laundry or crossword puzzles have been the main reasons thus far.

This year, Orrie is deep in the middle of some sort of monumental litigation, so it's up to Duet and me to decide if we want to attend the fair. We (that is, I) have determined that yes, we do indeed want to go. We want to go badly. And go we do. We eat massive amounts of blue cotton candy. Duet bounces on castles and we get our fortune told by a sixteen-year-old with way too much blue eye shadow. To top it all off, Duet and I stay in a local hotel that charges us a lot of money so we can pretend to be tourists. Perfect day so far.

And perfect it continues to be until we wait in line for forty minutes to enter the "trailer of terror." I, as parent, ask Duet if she really wants to go. I, as parent, look for any sort of disclaimer. I, as parent, ask the staff person at the entrance if this will be appropriate for a five year old. I, as parent, am told it will be fine. It will be perfectly fine to enter the trailer of terror.

What is terror, anyway?

Well, as it ends up – terror is kind of scary. Not just for Duet, but for me as well. There is a portion of the eight minute journey that is completely dark. You have to feel your way through the maze, step onto a gelatinous floor (yes, probably a water mattress), and touch a furry something-or-other on the wall (yes, probably pieces of an old teddy bear). But the not knowing what was going to happen, or the not knowing what you were going to bump into, and the basic intensity of not knowing, were terrifying.

Two seconds into it, Duet wants to go back. Three seconds into it, there is no way to go back because there is an exceedingly long line of people behind us, denying any possibility of navigating in that direction. The only route is forward. Duet gets to close her eyes and listen to me lie to her that everything is going to be okay. I pick her up, clutching her tightly to my chest. I lurch on the slippery floor, shuddering as I try to right myself on the furry wall. Ten seconds into it, Duet starts whimpering. I realize she's going to have nightmares. Orrie is going to be completely ticked at me for making such a bad decision. There's no air in here. I struggle to catch my breath. I try to calmly hum a comforting tune so Duet won't pee on me with fright. Eleven seconds into it, I just keep going, waiting for something worse and worse to happen. And it just keeps going. Not knowing. Just going. Not knowing. More jelly under your feet. More freaky fur on the wall to guide us.

And then it's over. I buy Duet a really large ice cream cone and hold her really tight, telling her this was a lesson she had to learn. I told her it might be scary, and that she still wanted to do it, and that it isn't my fault she was scared, and that this is a lesson, and she should listen, and that listening is good, and that she should listen, and that – and that ... what? That I made a bad choice? And now I'm trying to blame my child for it?

We walk back to the hotel, taking the long route along the waterway so we can have nice things to look at before going to bed. I tell Duet I'm sorry I let her go through the exhibit, and I made a bad decision.

"But why didn't you know, Mommy? Shouldn't you have known it would be too scary?"

"Sometimes mommies make mistakes, Du."

"Really?" I imagine her mind is conjuring up a different kind of fear. Mommies are supposed to know everything.

I finish my dripping ice cream cone, licking the stickiness off of my fingers. "Yep, but that's okay. Nobody is perfect. Even mommies. Even me. That's a good thing."

She tilts her head to the side. "Why?"

"Because we're not supposed to be perfect. We're human. Humans aren't perfect. We can still love and appreciate each other even though we make mistakes sometimes."

"I love you, Mommy."

I grab her and swing her around. "I love you too, Duet."

She giggles with glee and tumbles to the ground. I lie down beside her on the cool grass. She contemplatively picks at a piece of clover. "You love me even though I'm not perfect?"

"Of course. But I have to say that you are pretty darn close to perfection, though."

And that is that. We talk a bit more. We laugh a lot more. And then we watch a crap-load of cartoons back at the hotel. As I drift off to sleep with the TV still on, I think we had a pretty great day. Even though it wasn't absolutely perfect.

"Duet?" I quietly murmur before I start dreaming.

"Yes, Mommy?" she mumbles into her pillow. I inch close to her on the bed, moving the covers around so no air pockets will let in a chill. She begins to softly snore.

"Duet, do you ever talk to Colin? Can you see him sometimes?" I whisper, holding my breath.

She doesn't acknowledge my question and goes on snoring. I snuggle up beside her. If I hold her any closer, we would start bonding by diffusion. I put my hand over her heart, feeling the little patter patter patter patter it makes while pumping out blood to her body. She wiggles around, and I love the fact she's never truly still, she's always moving in some way, even when she's completely asleep.

I look up at the shadows on the ceiling, and for some reason, I stick my hand up so I'm pointing to them. *Are you there, Colin? Are you watching over us? Do you ever talk to Duet? Do babies and young children really see angels? Are you an angel, Colin? Do babies become angels?* I suppose, strictly in the religious sense, they don't. Humans and angels are separate creatures created by God. I like to think of Colin as an angel, though. I can even see his wings. I move my hand so it's no longer in the air anymore and let it sluggishly dangle over the side of the bed. I'm almost asleep when I feel like there's someone holding it. I keep my eyes closed and smile, leaving my hand hanging so I can have that feeling all night long. And for the first time in months, I sleep straight through until the next morning.

CHAPTER 43

It's a really crappy day outside. I hate driving in weather like this – too many opportunities to slither across the wet grease of the pavement, or get mired in one of the rivers rapidly developing on the highway with the deluge of rain coming down. I remember one time when I was young, I went outside to shower in rain like this. The shampoo and conditioner easily rinsed away in the nature-powered rain-shower.

I'm busy telling Duet this story, when she interrupts me and points out the car window. "Mommy, there's a car out there."

"Yes, of course, honey. We're on the road." I look around, but I actually don't see any other cars. It's pretty dead out this evening. I guess others share my hatred of driving in this kind of weather too. "We'll be home soon, sweetie. We're just a bit outside of town."

"No, Mommy. Not on the road. It's upside down back there. I saw it."

"Back where?" I ask, beginning to become alarmed. I look in my rearview mirror, but I still don't see any cars.

"It's in the ditch."

"Are you sure?" I ask, assuming she is pretending. I'm already preparing to tell her that she shouldn't make up stories that aren't funny or appropriate. I don't see any cars on the road, upside down or otherwise.

"It's back there, Mommy," she says while trying to point behind her, mildly strangling herself with her seatbelt in the attempt.

"Duet, I'm going to turn around to see. It's not good to make up these things."

"I'm not. It's back there. I'm sure, Mommy, I'm sure. I'm not pretending."

I slow down, peering around to see if it's possible to do a U-turn. It looks safe enough, so I carefully maneuver the car until I'm finally pointed in the other direction. I look in my rearview mirror again to make sure no one is behind me, and slowly creep back to the spot where Duet directs me.

"It's right there, Mommy. Do you see?"

And I do see it. Through the downpour, in the twilight, I see a small, blue hatchback on its roof with its headlights on, the lights shining through the fog and reflecting off the puddles in the ditch. I can't believe I didn't see it before. I pull our car off the road to park on the shoulder and put on my four-way flashers.

I fumble around my purse for my phone. "Duet, I need to you stay here, okay? I need to make a call and take a look." She promises to be very, very quiet while I call 911. I'm still in the car while I start reporting the incident and my location to the dispatcher. I calmly open the door with my shaky hand and get out into the storm. I look both ways before crossing the street to make my way to the vehicle. I hear the music coming from the car. It sounds like country, or maybe folk. The dispatcher wants to know if there's anyone in the car.

I tell him about the music and notice the lights are still on. He asks again if I know if anyone is in the car. I see a wet book lying beside the car. It's an alphabet book for toddlers. I tell him I don't know yet, but I'm going to look inside. I tell him that, all along, I've been yelling "hello" but no one has answered yet. I lick the top of my lip. It's salty. I don't know if the rain mixed with my sweat, or if I'm crying. It doesn't matter anyway. I have to look in the car. I tell the dispatcher there's a children's book outside the car, but I don't hear any kids. I don't hear any parents, either. All I hear is the wind and the rain and that stupid music. I can't see anyone inside through the windows because there's so much mud and rain. I tell the dispatcher it looks empty inside. I try to open the front door but it won't budge. It's then that I notice the backseat window is half open. I put my phone in my pocket, get down on all fours, and prepare to look in. But before I do, I actually cup my hands together to pray that everything will be all right. *And if it isn't, God, help me not freak out. Help me properly do whatever the dispatcher tells me to. And please, please, please God. Don't let there be any children involved. Please, please, please.*

I look in the car and it's empty. Completely empty and bloodless. It's actually tidier than my car, even though it's upside-down with a pocket of water gathering inside the roof. I yell another "hello" into the car, just to be sure. I need to be sure. I back my head out of the car and sit in the puddle, fishing my phone back out of my pocket.

"It's empty," I tell the dispatcher, unnecessarily yelling into the phone. He tells me that clean-up is on its way, the driver has just reported the accident, and they're okay. I see the lights of the emergency vehicles coming along to save me and the empty car. I run back to Duet to make sure we're together when they arrive.

"Everything okay, Mommy?"

"Yes, everything is okay. No one's hurt, everything is okay."

"Is anyone in the car?"

"No, I don't know where they are. But they're safe and everything will be okay. I was worried, though."

"Worried about what?" she asks.

I don't want to disclose what my mind horrifically envisioned was in the car. Instead, I say I was worried about what could have been, but wasn't. I was worried things wouldn't be okay, but they are going to be. And then, for the first time in a very long time, I mutter a prayer of thanks. *Thanks for nothing, God.* And I really, really mean that in the most appreciative way.

CHAPTER 44

"Have you been to playgroup lately?" Orrie asks, leaning on the kitchen cupboard.

"No, I can't find the time for it," I reply as I clean out the cat litter.

"But you never used to miss it, ever."

I wipe my forehead in the crook of my arm so the dirty rubber glove won't make contact with my skin. "Yeah, I don't know where the time goes."

"Are you avoiding it?"

"No," I lie. There is a part of me that aches to get back into the hallowed halls of the community center where I used to meet up with about ten other mothers from around town. Unfortunately, that part of me is buried underneath my chicken liver, and I can't get through all of the emotional bile.

Playgroup used to be where I delved into my motherdom. It was my coven where I reaffirmed my life choices. It confirmed my beliefs that staying home with my daughter was the right decision for me. Most of my friends don't even have children yet, and the ones that do have decided to go back to work. They never voice it, but sometimes I feel like I ruined their menagerie of superwomen. Staying home to them would have meant confinement and defeat. They don't understand how I can deal with a child full time without going buggy. After I decided that I would be a stay at home mom, I tried to explain I had never been happier, but they just nodded blankly, patting me on the head. In their world, I have given up. They think it must be so nice to be so lazy.

Playgroup was different.

Outside of the group, I didn't know any of the women who took part. To me, they were simply mothers and were defined as such. I've never been burdened to think of their lives or dreams. I loved the fact that we sat and discussed sugar-free alternative cooking and how best to potty train. They didn't even exist in my mind outside of that hour a day when we met. They were like my personal, interactive movie. The ultimate domestic video game. They weren't my friends or colleagues – they were my playgroup, and they belonged to me.

That being said, I now don't want to bring my life back into the fold. None of the women would probably know what happened to me, and I want to keep it that way. I don't want to explain my absence. I don't want to justify why I'm not pregnant anymore, or why I'm not bringing a new baby to the group. I just want to talk about tantrums and all of the superficial important things in life. I don't want to talk about life itself. I want to talk about the proper installation of car seats. I don't want to talk about what happens when the car seat fails in an accident and your child is flung amongst the chaos of coins and diapers that are flailing about in the crash. That's not part of my playgroup portrait.

I remember one woman told us about her recent miscarriage. We all felt terrible for her and had a discussion about it while the kids ran around our knees. Even as we were comforting her, I remember wondering what she did wrong. Did she not eat properly? Did she jog too much during her pregnancy? How could something so awful happen for no reason? I wanted to blame her so I would feel more secure. Blame is good for shielding yourself against catastrophes. My past judgment is my present damnation. I'm afraid others will feel that way about me. I don't want to deal with the irony. I don't want to go to playgroup and be condemned for being a bad mother because I never carried my son to term. That he never survived. That he died. I recognize the blame. I used it as a cushion myself. I just don't want to be someone else's security blanket.

I hear Orrie's voice. "Are you listening to me?"

"Of course," I respond, mildly annoyed at the accusation, even though I have no idea what he's talking about.

"So when are you going back?" Orrie asks, apparently for the second time.

"Back where?"

"To the group – the parenting group you used to go to."

"I'm not sure, I might not bother. Duet didn't get along with a couple of the kids very well, so I was thinking of not returning." I'm pleased with the lie I fabricate on the spot. I'm hopeful it will effectively put an end to the conversation.

Orrie leans back and crosses his arms. "You never mentioned that before."

"You never asked about it. Why? Do you think I'm lying?" I dart my eyes back and forth, giving myself away.

"Of course not," Orrie lies in return. He waits a few minutes. "Are there other groups you can join?"

I put my hand on my hip, forgetting about the dirty gloves. "Why? You want to ensure the house is routinely empty for any reason I should know about?"

Orrie rolls his eyes. "It would be nice if you could fit it back into your routine. Routine is good. You should also get out more. The house can't possibly be cleaner. My head is starting to hurt from the bleach. There's no need to thoroughly disinfect the bathroom every day, you know."

I gently kick him on the shin. "And if I didn't, you'd be complaining that I'm a slob. Besides, Gloria is the one who uses the bleach and does most of the housework. Did you want me to talk to her about it?"

Orrie looks at me and frowns. "Am I really so bad?"

"No, of course not." I take off my rubber gloves and give him a quick hug. "You're right, I should go. Maybe I'll go there tomorrow."

"But what about the kids Duet didn't get along with?"

"She's going to have to learn sometime that she has to face her fears."

"Good point."

Yes.

Yes, it is.

I decide to check out a support group for parents who have experienced early infant death. It's not the same as playgroup, but at least it gets me out of the house and Orrie out of my hair. Orrie says he'll take care of child care arrangements each week if Gloria isn't available. I was going to ask my mother to look after her, but Orrie feels it would be best if we just keep this to ourselves. *It's private. There's no need for anyone to know.* He believes there's a stigma associated with anything involving chairs arranged in a circle. I ask Orrie if he wants to go, but he says he's too busy. I feel if he can afford to take time off to look after Duet, then he can take the time to go to therapy. He just shrugs it off and says I can fill him in with the details when I get home. Maybe I'll ooze out epiphanies and wisdom on my return. In the end, Gloria offers to watch Duet while I go to my "meetings."

Do I even want to go? There's something itching for me to be involved with others who have had similar experiences, but I'm scared I'll break out in a rash after I'm exposed to them. I'm so used to not talking about what happened that I don't know what I'll do when I'm expected to participate.

How will I participate?

Will I participate?

How will I play with my new group?

I head out the next day to start my new intermingling. I'm usually early for everything. I actually get anxious if I arrive late for a date with friends or family. So when I arrive twenty minutes late for group, I can't believe how calm I am as I enter the brick community center. Brick. I love brick – it's so sturdy and secure. Sturdy, secure and solid. The building is red. Red is the color of blood. Sturdy, secure, solid bloody building.

Maybe I shouldn't bother going in if I'm so late. I can turn around any moment. I have that power. There are four steps to climb to the entrance. The paint is chipped on the door. Could that mean something? Is this a sign that I shouldn't go? There has to be a sign here somewhere ...

I don't want to be here.

There's no need for me to be here.

I'm sturdy.

I'm secure.

I'm solid.

I don't need group. I don't need this building.

I keep walking.

The corridor's floor is cold. My feet don't actually touch it, but I can sense through my sneakers that it's freezing like marble, even though it's cheap linoleum.

Room number 2312. That's me. That's them. That's the group. Am I the group once I go past the door? If I don't go through the door, can I still go home and honestly tell Orrie that I went to group? *Yeah, I was there but I didn't participate. I don't think I'll bother going again. I got what I needed. You don't have to make any more arrangements, sweetie. Thanks, though.*

The door creaks when I open it. Five women look up at me. None of them look like they've been crying or anything. There's a box of tissues sitting on one of the chairs, just in case. If the room wasn't so sterile, I might feel like I've walked into a wake. Funeral parlors are always much nicer, though. This is something entirely different. The furniture isn't as decadent.

"Avril?"

"Hello, that's me. I'm Avril. Sorry I'm late."

"No worries, please come in."

CHAPTER 45

I've gotten into the habit of taking Duet into bed with me whenever Orrie works late. We read stories and cuddle. She falls asleep in the bed and I doze off too. I've been telling Orrie that Duet is having nightmares and doesn't want to sleep in her own room. I don't even feel guilty about misleading (outright lying) to him. I know I shouldn't do this, but I don't want to stop. If I tell him the truth, it will just become an issue that I don't want to bother with.

I wonder if I'll bring this up in group. I wonder if it's something that anyone else in group is going through. Maybe we should call ourselves a flock. A flock of bitterness, sadness, regret and hope. I wonder how long people go to group before they feel it's time to fly away and find a new flight pattern.

Group isn't as nerve-wracking as I thought it would be. I pictured it like the AA meetings I see on TV.

Hi, I'm Avril.

Hi, Avril.

Hi, I'm Avril and I don't have a baby.

Hi, Avril.

It's been many, many days since I last had a baby.
Hi, Avril.

My group is more like a living room chat with a group of strangers that you've known intimately all of your life. Sometimes it's like listening to your mirror image with your eyes closed. Sometimes I don't even pay attention, and I let my mind wander to Duet and Colin. I see them playing on the checkered floor, Duet running circles around the drooling, burping baby. Then I gap back into the group to hear how everyone else is dealing with their journey to the magical land of Recovery.

I take my travel mug full of decaf coffee with me to the community center for my next meeting. It's Denise's turn to lead the sharing exercise today. Denise has been going to group for about two weeks. Her baby was a boy, as well. They named him Trevor. After Denise was induced, Trevor never made it past the birth canal, and was stillborn.

When I first had Colin, I remember wondering if he was stillborn. I needed the doctor to tell me he was alive. I never, ever saw my son move. I couldn't even see his belly go up and down. He just was. He was still. He was born. I decide not to share this observation with Denise.

Denise is the embodiment of venomous bitterness. She hooks her vitriol to her previous employer who royally screwed her around. Denise tells us she had worked for a small family business that was just starting to expand. She worked there for around seven years. Even though it had its problems, she stuck with it, putting in her eight-hour days plus overtime when it was called for. She was so excited when she found out she was pregnant. She really wanted to have a little playmate for her son who was just about to turn eleven. She knew they wouldn't be hanging out as peers, but she was excited her son would have a little brother or sister. Losing her baby was gut-wrenching, but she felt she was never actually hurt so much as when she was told by her employers that they were going to cut off her healthcare benefits if she took a maternity leave.

"Losing Trevor was the most painful experience of my life," she says. "But they hurt me in a way I never knew before. They hurt me on purpose to save money."

"Is that legal?" someone asks.

I'm about to chime in with what I remember from law school when Denise responds. "Apparently not. I fought it. There was precedent, or something. I didn't even have to go to court. But that doesn't even matter so much as the fact that the guy who decided this, Jeremy Bickens, was someone I saw every day and said hello to. It wasn't a computer program that randomly picked my name from a list and sent me a blind email. He made the conscious decision to do that to me."

"Did you kill him?" A lady in a checkered shirt demands as she looks around the room. "I'd kill him."

"No. But the kicker is that a month after this happened, he was appointed to president of the company. The CEO of the company, Jonathan Billboy, wrote me an email stating he was sorry for the way his staff handled things. Yeah, he was sorry enough to promote a colon-dweller like Jeremy."

The woman in the checkered shirt is getting very agitated. I wonder if she's planning on hunting Jeremy down after our group session is over. Her name is June. I might have to remember that for the police report if she does anything serious.

"I never respected him," Denise continues, "but now I hate him so much it keeps me awake at night." Denise starts to bawl. She holds it together with dignity and composure when talking about her baby dying, but her eyes lose it completely when she discusses her workplace experience.

"Maybe you hate them because you can't get angry at Trevor," someone new from the circle offers.

"No, it's beyond that. I've thought of that. I hate them so much because they deliberately did something unbelievably cruel. I received the email from work exactly one week after Trevor died. I was still grieving and recovering from twelve hours of labor. I expected a card of sympathy from work, not an email informing me that they were cutting off my healthcare."

"Wow," we all chime in, sympathetically.

"And Jeremy," she says his name like she is spitting out cancer, "He told my husband it wasn't anything personal; it was just business. My husband said we were taking it very personally, indeed."

"Wow," we all repeat.

"So, did you end up getting your healthcare?" a woman named Patty asks.

"Yeah, but that wasn't the issue. I just couldn't believe they would do something like that, especially so soon after my baby died. Trevor dying was a tragedy. What they did was a deliberate act of cruelty. It felt personal."

Patty leans forward in her chair. "So are you going to sue them?" she inquires, almost hopefully.

"I talked to a lawyer about it, but there's nothing that can be done."

"That's unbelievable."

"Yep, so all I have are my confrontation fantasies where I slap him across the face or scream at him. It's eating me up inside. I can't grieve because I'm so angry. They've even taken that away from me."

"Maybe you need to talk to someone," a lady in an orange chair suggests.

Denise looks around the room. "That's what I'm doing right now."

"I'd kill him," June, the checkered lady, repeats. "I really would."

"No," Denise mutters with hesitation, "He's not worth it. Not really."

June wiggles in her seat. "I would find a way to kill him slowly. Find out where he regularly buys his coffee and put something in it each day. Do something to his stomach so he would be in pain before he died."

Janet is next. "I found out my baby wasn't viable when I went for a routine ultrasound," she shares. "My husband hid around the corner so he could peek at the machine. I told myself not to look at the screen because it would be bad luck, but then I looked anyway." She shares that even though she rationally knows looking at the monitor didn't have a factor in the outcome, she will never be able to forgive herself for looking at the screen. She was hoping for twins, so when she saw just one form on the monitor, she remembers feeling disappointed. "The person who was doing the procedure looked a little perplexed. She left the room to request another person to look at the screen," Janet continues. "I asked her if anything was wrong, but she smiled at me and said it was normal procedure to get a second opinion on these things."

I tell Janet that the same thing had happened to me, but I didn't elaborate because interrupting someone else's story is against the rules. Janet didn't remember two separate people looking at the ultrasound when she went in for her other children, but she didn't question it. Her husband snuck in. Janet shared with him that she noticed on the monitor that they weren't having twins. He was visibly disappointed. Then the two attendants came back, looked over the screen, and meticulously moved the instrument over her slippery, full belly. *"Are you sure nothing is wrong?"* Janet asked. *"Yes, there is something wrong,"* the senior attendant said. *"There's something terribly wrong."*

"How do you respond to something like that?" Janet cries.

I tell the group that my technician told me Colin had no head. I recognize that I'm pushing it by putting in my two cents worth yet again, but everyone seems okay with my interruption, so I don't think I did anything disastrous. We talk for a bit about how we were told "the news", and how holes really do open up from underneath the ground to swallow your soul when you hear the words. It's one of the true metaphysical experiences in life that defy explanation. Your body still exists on the physical plane, but your ears can't hear what's going on because your soul is stuck in an underwater sewer system somewhere in another dimension and it's mucking up the sound system.

Flora tells us she had to wait a couple of days before she was induced.

"I had to wait almost a week," I pipe up. I remind myself that this is group, not a competition. *Stop it. Stop it.*

Iris is next to speak. I'm sure her story is interesting, but I never have any idea what she contributes to the conversation because she always talks with her mouth full. There are assorted snacks available for group members, and Iris constantly feels the need to stuff her face while she shares with the group. Every time I look over, I see nothing but the mushed-up pieces of white bread in her mouth. I am too appalled to listen to her.

After Iris finishes, we continue our rounds and expel our stories. Two hours pass, and after a while I wonder if I really want to be there anymore. In the end, as I retreat down the steps, I decide not. I never told my full story, but I think the meetings were beneficial – *yes, Orrie, you were right* – so I'm glad I went. I just don't think I need to keep going any more. I went three times, that's enough for me.

Later on, as I lie down with Duet, I think to myself that I have a much better therapy session at home, just listening to Duet breathe. There is nothing in this world more soothing. And after Orrie comes home, I wrap myself around him to nestle in cozy for the night. My blankets are my bandages. That's all I need for now.

CHAPTER 46

Joanie looks up at me. "So how about it?"

I shake my head. "I don't know ..."

"Well, there's no pressure."

"Yeah ..." I waver.

Joanie excitedly jumps up from the floor. "Oh, come on. There's just going to be a small group of us. We'll start out at my place and then we'll go dancing or something."

"I don't know," I repeat.

"It's just that no one has seen you in a while. It will be good for you to get out."

"Yeah, I know, I just don't know if I'm up for it."

"You have to go out sometime," Joanie insists. "This is the perfect opportunity to get your feet wet. Everyone here will be friends. There are no expectations."

I walk over to the kitchen. "I don't know if I'm ready to see a whole bunch of people yet. I don't know what to say."

Joanie follows me. "Everyone's worried about you," she reveals. "This will be a great opportunity to let everyone know that you're okay. You are okay, aren't you?"

I open the refrigerator, looking for a snack. "Yeah, I'm okay, I just don't know if I'm ready to talk in front of a group of people."

"Haven't you been going to group sessions to do just that?"

"That's different. And I don't think I'm going to go anymore, anyway." I close the fridge door.

"It's not like you'll be making a presentation. It's just going to be a group of friends in the comfort zone of my condo. We'll have some wine and chat, just like old times."

I take a bite out of a crunchy red apple. "But people will want to talk about it."

"They're not people, they're your friends," Joanie protests. "No one will want to talk about it if you don't want to. We just want to see you. We haven't seen you out in a very long time. You won't be expected to be the life of the party."

"Well, I never was before," I try to joke. "You forget I'm the quiet kid in the corner at all of your little soirees."

"So no one will even question if you don't feel like talking," she counters.

"I don't know ..."

"I do. You should come. Don't think of it as a party in your honor. It's not. I'm having people over whether you come or not, but it would be awesome if you are a part of it. It would be just like old times."

I feel like telling her that it's not like old times. The old times are as ancient and dead as Egypt's tombs. Instead I mumble, "Well, maybe."

"Like I said, I don't want to pressure you. But then again, maybe you should be pressured. You have to return to normal. It's not good to cocoon for too long."

"I'm not cocooning, I'm just laying low."

"You're basically non-existent. No one's seen you out in months. I don't even see you that often, and you're my sister who used to be a living fixture on my sofa. I need you to come; I miss you. Stop being so selfish," she chides.

"Okay, okay. I'll be there," I give in. "What time is everyone coming?"

"Around eight or so. You be here around six. Get a babysitter, or make Orrie stay home for a change."

"Orrie helps out quite a bit," I tell her. For a minute it does feel like old times with Joanie busting Orrie's chops. Joanie has always felt that Orrie doesn't do enough around the house.

"Well, if he's helping out more then he won't mind staying at home with Du for the night and letting you out."

"It's not a matter of 'letting me.' I just haven't felt like doing much lately."

"I know. But you have to get back on the horse and get moving. Life isn't stagnant."

"There's nothing stagnant about my life; I'm just not into seeing a lot of people. I don't feel like talking about it. It's weird."

"Colin is always going to be a part of your life. Are you going to ignore people until you die because you're afraid to talk about it?"

"I'm not afraid," I lie.

"Colin died, Avie. You didn't. You have to keep going."

"Keeping going involves drinking wine with the girls?"

"It's a part of it, yes."

"Well, I guess I better go then," I say, getting annoyed at her. Joanie is always an expert in things that she has no clue about.

"Don't go if you don't want to. I just want you to want to."

"Well, I don't."

"You should," she struggles.

"Okay, I'll go." I have no backbone. Besides, Joanie has won every single argument or confrontation that we've had since I started blinking. I might as well just give up.

"Great, I'll see you tomorrow. Don't cancel."

"Okay. See you then."

The night of the party, everyone is all sprawled out over Joanie's numerous sofas. The center table has a couple of lukewarm wine bottles sweating on the coasters. Our (Joanie's) friends mostly like cooled white wine, whereas I'm the rebel of the bunch and prefer a nice cheap merlot.

I think I'm on my third glass, and they've all been pretty hefty helpings. Joanie has beautifully ornate glasses that are bluish and see-through. I hold up the glass to my eyes, noticing a couple of air pockets trapped on the side. I wonder if they've been placed there on purpose, or if it's a flaw. Either way, it looks beautiful. Imperfection always has its place.

"Avie?"

"Hmmm?"

"How you doing? You're pretty quiet."

"Fine I am."

"What?"

"I'm fine," I correct myself and pretend to listen to what the group is saying. I study the faces of the others as they take turns talking about politics and various academic topics. I love it when people talk. It gives you the opportunity to really look at them. It's like a license to gape. Sharon's getting a bit wrinkled around the lips. She smokes too much. I look at her exhale and wonder if she realizes what it's doing to her smile. She catches me watching her and beams at me. I smile back then turn my gaze to the next talker.

I love wine. Wine. Wine. Wine. When you say it over and over again, it sounds like a word from another language. Wine. My butt is itchy. I wonder if I can politely scratch it. It doesn't matter, no one will notice. I get up to scratch my bum and spill my wine over the cushions. I look around to see if anyone witnessed my clumsiness, but they're too enraptured by a conversation about existentialism. I wonder what an existentialist would think about that. Actually, I wonder what an existentialist would think about me asking that question. I smudge the wine into the pillow, hoping it doesn't stain. Oh well, I don't care if anyone notices. Joanie can afford another pillow.

I look over at Joanie, and watch everyone else watching her. She's like a beam of electricity that everyone is drawn to. She's always been the one with the personality. I've been content to be her servant. Are things drawn to electricity, or is it magnets that things are drawn to?

Wi

ne.

I need more. I've spilled and drunk the last of my cup. It no longer runneth over.

"More wine, Avie?" Joanie asks.

"You just read my mind, sister."

"You better slow down, we're still going out after this."

"Then why did you ask if I wanted more?"

"Well, I'm not limiting you."

"Yes, I'll have more. I'm fine, pour away."

After we get home from the bar, I remember why I don't drink a lot anymore. I am so sick. I am going to throw up. I'm not going to make it to the bathroom. I'll just get sick here and clean it up in the morning. I can't believe I'm debating this. Maybe I should go to the bathroom to get sick there. I'm not going to make it to the bathroom. Joanie's going to kill me.

I don't make it to the bathroom.

I have to lie down again.

The next morning, I wake up to a throbbing headache. Alcohol truly is a depressant. You don't realize it until the next day when you're all oily and covered in emotional grime. While you're drinking, everything is rosy and full of id, but the next day, the superego awakens and starts to click off every single stupid thing that you did the night before, and you get depressed even if there's nothing embarrassing to tick off. I tumble out of bed, wobbling to the living room. Joanie beams at me from the couch. "Did I do anything stupid?" I croak.

Joanie's smile broadens. "No, of course not."

"Are you sure? I'm pretty certain I started crying."

"Yeah, you might have, but everyone understands."

"I cried in the bar, didn't I?" I ask, red blotches still stamped all over my face.

"Yeah, but no one noticed except us."

"Of course others saw. I feel like such an idiot."

"Don't be silly. Did you have a good time?"

I stare at her, speechless. "No. I wish I didn't go out. I could be home with Duet and without a headache right now."

"It's good you went out. It's the first step. The next time will be easier."

I flop down on the couch, my arms crossed. "There won't be a next time."

"Yes, there will. Don't worry about having a little cry. Everyone else would have done the same thing."

"I just wish I never went out."

"Don't be silly."

I rub my eyes. "What time is it?"

"Twelve thirty. Want to go for lunch? It's on my credit card. I'm buying if you're going."

"As long as it's really greasy and unhealthy."

"That's my girl," Joanie squeals.

"Shhh, not so loud. I'm recuperating."

"Sorry. When do you want to go?"

"Just give me a moment to collect myself. Did anyone else crash over?"

"No, just you. Orrie called this morning. He wanted to see how you were doing. He and Duet are fine, so you don't have to hurry home. I think he's enjoying the alone time."

I rest my head on a fuzzy couch pillow. "Did Duet mind going to bed without me?"

"He didn't mention it, so I doubt it. It sounds like they're having a great time."

"Nice to know I'm not needed," I grumble.

"Let's get some omelets that are covered with cheese," Joanie suggests.

"Okay, I just have to wash my face and change my clothes. These reek of cigarette smoke. You really shouldn't let people smoke in your home."

"It doesn't bother me. Besides, I smoke. I just air out the house the next day. It's not like I have kids to worry about."

I fully lie back on the sofa. "Do you think you'll ever have kids, Joanie?"

"I don't need to, I have you and Duet. Plus, don't forget our brothers. There's the terrible twins' kids."

I sit up. "Don't you ever want your own family, though?"

"Don't be silly. You're my own family. Now - wash your face. I want to go," Joanie swiftly responds, conveniently ignoring my real question. "Do you need to borrow any clothes?"

"No, I have some in my bag. I shouldn't take long."
I walk down the corridor and remember that I had an accident last night. "Sorry I puked on your floor," I yell to Joanie.

"No problem. I've handled worse."

I get to the bathroom and am shocked at the ravages of my reflection. I never used to look this way. Ten years ago, I could stay out all night, splash a bit of water on my eyes the next day, and be as fresh as a daisy. Now I could knock someone over with a glance.

It's going to be a long, long, long day.

After lunch, I get home to an empty house and a note that says Orrie and Duet went for a walk and won't be home for a while. I still feel full from the restaurant, but nevertheless, I grab a bag of chips from the cupboard and dump them in a bowl to munch on while I gap out on the couch.

I hate drinking.

I hate the emptiness that follows a night of binging and idiocy. I eat a couple more chips and decide to have a shower to get some of the grime off me. I never want to drink again. It's a silly habit that just doesn't jive with my life. I cried in the bar last night. I'm such an idiot.

I hate drinking.

I wonder if I'll ever see anyone again from the bar last night. If I did, I wouldn't remember who they were, but I'm sure that they'd remember me. *"See that woman? She's the one I was telling you about. You know, the one who was crying. Issues, issues, issues."* I hate the fact that life is so completely linear and irreversible. You never have the ability to take back things you do or say. Everything matters. Everything is permanent. You never escape your actions. You never escape your consequences. There's no delete button. There's no editing. You just keep living, hoping everything will be fine. For the rest of eternity, I will have cried in that bar last night. And in the grand scheme of things, it really doesn't matter, because in the grand scheme of things, *I* don't really matter. But on the Avril scheme of things, it is a big deal. Forever, it will be an event I'll be ashamed of. I'll always cringe at the thought that I broke down in a bar full of strangers. It's even worse that I was drunk at the time. It makes it more pathetic and less genuine. I haven't cried in front of any of my friends when I was sober. Why should I make an event of it when I'm all sloshed and slurring? What would Colin think if he saw me? Would he want to be with me if he saw me acting in such a manner? Is that how a good mother behaves?

I hate drinking.

Do I like being me, though?

I search my psyche for the truest answer. I come up with a kernel of yes. Yes, I do. Or at least I don't hate me. I can like me, even if I'm an idiot. Because I'm also alive, surviving and ultimately getting better. Albeit, very, very slowly. But better, despite the multiple bumps along the way. I just don't like me all the time. And I'm going to try to accept that.

CHAPTER 47

The biggest things that happened to me today included Orrie not getting in a car accident, Duet not drowning in a pool, and me not slashing my face with a knife. Life is just as much about what doesn't happen as what does. Orrie thinks this is a very dangerous way to view life, but I think it's valid enough to think about.

Orrie didn't have triple bypass surgery.

My house didn't burn down.

My computer didn't crash.

I didn't trip over one of Duet's toys and bash my skull on the corner of the living room table.

Duet didn't fall down the stairs and break her collarbone.

An asteroid didn't fall from the sky and burn my community into the core of the earth.

I didn't leave the coffee pot plugged in when I went to the store, and my kitchen didn't catch on fire because the tea towel was too close to the burner.

Gloria didn't split her hand open when she was slicing tomatoes for a salad.

The neighborhood dog didn't bite through my door and rip my neck open in an attempt to get at Duet.

To the best of my knowledge, we're not in the middle of a nuclear war.

I didn't get pregnant this morning and my baby didn't die this afternoon because of a neural tube defect. Actually, that happened a couple of months ago. That did happen. I'm trying to be grateful for what didn't.

CHAPTER 48

Parents never truly sleep after they have a child. Or at least I haven't, even before Colin. I've always been on the verge of waking up for any emergency. It's the silent emergencies that scare me the most. My greatest fear in life is that I'll go to Duet's bed someday and she won't be breathing. There have been nights where I go over the scenario again and again in my mind, until I force myself over to her bed and put my hand on her belly to ensure there's movement. I've forever found that looking isn't enough. I need the touch in order to ensure another moment of slumber. I didn't even need a tragedy to have this irrational fear. Before Duet turned a year old, I usually went over to her crib three or four times a night. She never even moved out of our room until she was two years old. I wanted to be able to hear her breathe beside me. Orrie finally put his foot down, telling me I was being unreasonable. Even though I agreed, it still hurt to see her move down the hall. Now I feel like I'm raiding her privacy when I sneak in during the middle of the night. Maybe I am irrational. Maybe

I'm even an invader. Maybe I'm the boogeyman who won't let my daughter sleep.

I'm in the middle of thinking how I'm going to have to grow up (and let her grow up) when I hear something rustle down the hall. I excitedly/ashamedly throw down the covers in the hopes that she's had a nightmare and I'll get to comfort her. I look over at my still sleeping husband. I telepathically promise I'll get better. I'll just wait until tomorrow to do so. Or at least next week. Or next month. I promise. But then Orrie stirs, so I stay in bed in case he wakes up.

When I was young, I used to be afraid of monsters. Monsters and fire. I have no specific idea how the monsters crept into my subconscious, but I remember seeing a movie when I was young about a village that caught fire. It left an impact that just wouldn't unstick. Each night, I alternated between the two fears. It was like a clock ticking back and forth between sheer terror and petrification. Tick: the creatures dwelling in the shadows. Tock: the wood stove blowing up, engulfing my family in flames. My mother was always there to comfort me and tell me everything would be all right. It was so incredibly comforting to put my nose in her collarbone, smell her perfume, and believe her fairy tales of happiness ever after. I want to be young. Even more so, I ache for my mother to have that power again. I wonder if my mom lied to me. Did she ever believe things would work out for the best? Did my mom mislead me? And if she didn't, when did she change into someone who couldn't solve the earth's problems and keep all of the world's monsters at bay? When did she become human?

It is two o'clock in the morning and all is unwell. I hear Duet talking in her sleep, so I go to her room, picking her up to stash her in my bed. She easily falls into a deep sleep between Orrie and me. It's not right that I use her to comfort me. I need to stop depending on her to make myself feel better. I'm supposed to be her knight in shining armor, not the other way around. It's too much of a burden to place on a child. It's not fair. I have to stop. I have to.

The streetlight outside our window casts a glow on Duet's head. I look over at her dreaming peacefully under the covers. I count her eyelashes and touch her cheek. She stirs a little. I'm scared that I've woken her, but she rolls over, nuzzles against Orrie's arm, and goes back to her night-time adventures. I turn back towards the wall, wondering what she dreams of at night. Do her teddies have tea parties after she goes to sleep? Does she fly in her dreams? I used to have flying dreams all the time. It was fantastic. Now I dream of dead kittens and car accidents. I don't know which is worse – not sleeping, or having nightmares. It's a really lousy cycle I've crept into. I wonder what my mother would do if I called her this late at night.

I look over and am shocked to see Orrie staring at me. "Can't sleep?" he whispers.

"Yes. I mean, no. No, I can't sleep."

"Want me to go downstairs to make some hot milk for you?"

"No, that's okay. Thanks, though."

"I can put some honey in it."

"No."

"I don't mind."

"Well, okay."

"You can come too."

"But then Duet would be all alone in the bed. She might fall out and hurt herself."

"That's not going to happen."

"She might hit her head on the night stand on the way down," I continue.

"She'll be fine. Don't worry."

"Maybe we should take her into her own bed," I suggest.

He traces his thumb along the side of my face. "But she might fall out of her own bed," he quietly jokes.

I scoop our daughter up in my arms, taking her into her own bed. I cover her up in her sheets so she won't get cold, and kiss her a midnight goodnight. By the time I get to the kitchen, the boiling milk is steaming happily on the stove.

"Why aren't you sleeping?" Orrie inquires.

"I don't know. I just can't. I'm wound up."

"Over what?"

"I honestly don't know."

"Are you having nightmares again?"

"Yeah, sometimes. Less than before, though."

Orrie stirs the milk and I watch the bubbles playfully expanding to the rim of the pot. "What do you dream about?" I ask.

"I don't usually dream."

"Really?"

"Well, I guess I must dream of something. I just don't remember anything when I wake up. I don't know if I'm lucky or cursed. It would be kind of depressing if I was having all of these really cool experiences I couldn't remember," he says.

"But what if you're having bad dreams? Then you're having all of these weird, horrible images in your mind that you're never aware of. I wonder what that's doing to your psyche."

"Who knows," he contends as he takes the pot over to the cupboard and pours me a cup. "I guess I can only assume the images are good. That way I can be happy about it."

"Or sad that you can't remember them."

"It all depends on how you look at it. My way is more positive than yours."

"True," I agree as I take a sip. Orrie looks hard at me, gets up from his chair, and ruffles my messy hair. "You know everything is going to be alright, don't you?" he breathes into my scalp.

I nuzzle my face into his chest and inhale his cologne. I think for a moment, breathing deeply. "Yeah, I guess I do."

The next morning, Orrie kisses me and tells me that he'll be back in a bit. I go to sleep for another hour or so before Duet jumps in my bed, demanding breakfast. We're just about to eat when I hear the doorbell ring. I'm surprised to see Orrie standing on the front step.

"Why are you ringing the bell?" I ask.

"I have a surprise," Orrie responds excitedly.

"What is it?"

"A puppy."

"What?" I shout, even though he's inches away.

"A dog."

"You got a what?"

"A dog, Avril. I got it for Duet."

"A puppy!" Duet squeals from the hallway. Her squeak gets louder and louder until she's at the front door with Orrie and me, and then she just starts quivering all over with delight. "Is he ours, Daddy? Is he mine?"

Orrie looks at me. "If you want him, Du, he's yours."

Duet leaps up and down, rattling the paintings in the hallway. "Careful, Duet," Orrie laughs. "Stop jumping and I'll put the puppy down beside you."

"I want to call him Colin," Duet gushes as the puppy licks her face. Orrie and I quickly look at each other.

"He already has a name, sweetie," Orrie says. "His name is Penelope."

"That's an odd name for a boy." I jump back as the little beast tries to sniff my feet.

"That's because he's a she," Orrie laughs as he picks up the dog and touches noses with it.

"Mine, mine," Duet yelps from below. "Put her down." Orrie squeezes the puppy and passes the squirming ball of fur to Duet, but not before it pees all over the floor from mid-air.

"You're cleaning that up," I command. "That is your mess."

"It's not a mess, it's a pet. And she's awesome. Every kid should have a dog. I had a dog. Didn't you have a dog?"

"You know I don't like dogs. I was bitten by a dog. Don't you even remember? I needed twelve stitches." I pull my hair back so he can see the lumpy scar. "I've never liked dogs."

"Maybe the dog sensed your resentment, and that's why the dog bit you," Orrie grins. I glare back, but soften a little when I see how overjoyed Duet is.

"Well, you have to clean out the litter box," I tell Orrie.

"Dogs don't have litter boxes."

"You know what I mean. And if he eats any – and I mean ANY – of my personal items, then you have to be the one to tell Duet he's leaving."

"He is a she. And I'll take full responsibility."

"Orrie, I'm not being unreasonable. I have a scar," I repeat, pulling my hair back again.

"It will be fine," Orrie promises.

"You have to walk him."

"I'll walk her every day. And I'll buy the dog food, and I'll train her. You wait, Avie. You're going to love her."

"We'll see," I sigh. I tug at my hair, knowing he's utterly, completely, totally wrong.

CHAPTER 49

I'm over at Joanie's as she gleefully looks over a bounty of presents she received from colleagues at her work. Last week was her five-year anniversary with her company. Her workmates organized a surprise party and everyone brought a beauty product as a gift. Apparently, this is the first time anyone has ever had an anniversary party held for them. Even as an adult, Joanie is still the popular cool kid everyone adores.

Joanie takes out a brown mascara sample, handing it to me. "You should use this. It will accentuate your lashes without being too bold."

I push it away. "No thanks, I don't do mascara."

"You should, it would look nice. Let me put some on you."

I shake my head and she pouts. "Not going to work, Joanie. I don't want to put it on, I'll look silly."

"Everyone wears mascara, Avie. It's not like a face tattoo."

"No."

"Please?"

"Why do you care if I use your stuff? Besides, it would be a waste. You wouldn't be able to wear it after I do, it would be unhygienic."

"It's a sample. And it's brown. I haven't worn brown mascara since the sixth grade."

"Can I put some on?" Duet begs from my knees.

"No, sweetie. It would poke you in the eye and hurt. Besides you don't need it."

"No one *needs* it, Avie." Joanie moans. "It's fun. It's not necessary."

Duet is already bored with our conversation. She goes over to play with her toys that are permanently stored at Joanie's for her visits. I guess adult dress-up sounds dull and possibly painful. Plus, she's used to Joanie and me bickering back and forth for hours, so best to leave early and play on her own.

"Just let me put a bit on, you won't even notice."

"So why bother then?"

"It will be fun."

"Nope."

"It will be fun for me. You owe me."

"For what?"

"For being an amazing sister."

"You're an *annoying* sister."

"Please?"

"Fine." I sit in front of Joanie like a rag doll and let her put the mascara on me. She directs me to open my mouth and eyes as wide as I can so she can apply the brown sludge properly. When she finishes, I look in the mirror and am not amazed at the results. "It doesn't look any different."

"I told you that it wouldn't," Joanie explains.

"So why did we do this?"

"I just wanted to see."

I hang out at Joanie's for another hour and then scoop up Duet to get going. We've been invited to a party. It's the same crew from the *orange pee incident*, so I'm assuming either they don't know what happened, or they are very forgetful. Either way, once I get there, the conversation is just as painful as it was before. Mostly it's me moving from circle to circle, smiling and chewing food while people talk to each other. I don't really know anyone here. I'm not sure why I put myself in these awkward social situations. Do I even want Duet to hang out with these children? Are they nice? Is it worth it?

I look over at the owner's private pool and see Duet and a couple of girls venturing into the water without any swimming devices or supervision. Excitedly, I tell no one who is listening that I'll be back - I should just go with the kids in the pool to make sure everyone is safe. Everything is fine and fun for the next twenty minutes, and then it's time to get out for a rest. I haul Duet with me and am about to go up the steps when I see Jimmy Simms coming towards me. He was the cutest guy in my entire high school. And he looks just as delicious as he ever did. Better even, with gentle gray hairs tangled into his sandy blond mane.

My entire body goes numb and I am awash with horror. I quickly entice Duet back into the pool, heading towards the deeper end where my body is safely hidden in the chlorine cover-up. I am at least thirty pounds heavier than when I last saw Jimmy. I would rather die than have him see me in my unflattering mom bathing suit that is pasted to my belly button in the most disgusting way possible. And I didn't bother camouflaging my pasty dimples with a spray tan because this was a kid's party and I didn't feel any need to look good. There weren't supposed to be any high school hunks here.

I'm swishing around with Duet when he glides along with his twin boys. He holds up each child with his bulging, muscular arms. I try to smile, but my mouth is dry and my top lip sticks to my teeth. I turn around and lick it free in a panic. Duet asks me what's wrong, and I laugh loudly, confusing her.

"Avril? Is that you?"

I look back. "Oh, hi, Jimmy. Fancy seeing you here. I haven't seen you in a while. How are things?"

"Pretty good. That's my wife over there," he points to a blonde goddess with a perfect figure. "Her name is Annie."

"That's a nice name," I say, lamely.

"And these are my boys, Chuckie and Lucas."

"They look like you," I smile.

"How are your brothers doing? Are they still overseas?" he asks and we then catch up on what's been going on with each other's families over the past decade or so. Except one thing. I don't bring up Colin. I tell myself I don't need to share that detail.

Jimmy looks over at the patio. "Looks like it's time for cake." He starts to leave and notices I don't move. "Are you coming?"

"Yes, in a minute. I'm just going to go for a little swim with Duet. We both adore swimming. Can't get enough of it."

"No, Mommy, I'd like cake," Duet squeaks.

"We'll have cake, Sweetie. We'll just swim first. Let's let Jimmy, Chuckie and Lucas get out of the pool first. We don't want to all go in a rush."

A few minutes later, I determine the coast is clear. I rip out of the pool and quickly put on my clothes without even drying off. As we're about to join the group, Duet intently squints at me. "Mommy, you have something on your face."

I brush off my cheek. "Is it gone?" I ask.

"No, it's on your eyes. And under your eyes. And there's a little bit on your chin."

I tell Duet to wait on the chair while I rush to the washroom. And then I see the damage. I forgot about the mascara that Joanie made me put on earlier today. It's ferociously plastered all over my face. I was blissfully unaware of the carnage, in all my innocent glory, as I chatted with Jimmy. He was apparently too gracious to say anything. *Ugh, ugh, ugh.* I wash my face in the sink and look in the mirror again. "Let's go home, Sunshine," I mutter to myself. "It's time. Mask is off."

As I gather up Duet-to leave, I hear Jimmy yelling at me. "Hey, Avril – we have cake up here for you. Hurry up before the ice cream melts."

I try to think up an excuse to head out but am too tired to even try. Defeated, I head up to join everyone and get my cake. "You look different," Jimmy smirks. "Sorry I didn't mention anything."

"What's up?" his wife asks.

"Avril's mascara was running down her face when she was in the pool."

"Oh, I hate when that happens!" Annie laughs.

Jimmy grabs his wife in a hug and lovingly shakes her. "It happens to Annie all the time."

Other people hear our conversation and join in about their embarrassing pool events. As it turns out, there are many. People listen with gleeful delight, and it ends up being the best party I've been to in a long time. We stay well into the evening, and I hook up a couple play dates for Duet. I've been so busy trying to hide my imperfections that I forgot they're what make us human and relatable. I'll have to go to Joanie's tomorrow and pick up some more mascara.

And I'll use it. Not to hide, but to highlight.

CHAPTER 50

It's been ten months since Colin died, and each day I think of him a little less. I take this as an odd accomplishment in my healing. Sometimes it doesn't even seem like any of this ever happened to me.

> *Colin?*
> *Colin who?*
> *Oh, that little baby who died?*
> *That happened to the mother down the street.*
> *Just terrible.*
> *I feel bad for her.*
> *Poor thing.*

I mean, how can I feel whole when something has viciously ripped my soul? How can I be serene? How can I forget? I look at Colin's tree and crookedly smile at the ironic fact that I've spent more time with his tree than I did with him. I touch its leaves to pick off anything brown and crusty, letting it blow away from my hands. I talk to the tree without even caring if someone can hear me doing it.

"How are you today, Colinstree? Any nice birds pop by? Anything poop on you? Any new fertilizer? Yeah? That's cool. Duet made a picture of you today, I'll bring it out later."

I'm so comfortable with my insanity, it doesn't even feel insane. It cools my psyche like sweat on skin. Or maybe it's totally normal to talk to a tree that grows on the ashes of your baby. I have no idea. Maybe there's a forum out there somewhere I can consult.

It freaks me out that I'm not freaked out as much. Sometimes I make myself cry so I know I have feelings for him. I want to be aware that I'm still a bit raw from the experience. I need to know a bit of pus remains on my bandage. But why does any emotion dealing with Colin have to be painful? He was a beautiful little baby. He really was. Can't I think of him in my arms and smile because he was so wonderful? Can't I be merry because of Colin, not just in spite of him? When I recollect his little belly, shouldn't I smile because it was so round? When I think of his perfect tiny hands, shouldn't I beam with pride because they were the hands of my son? My son had beautiful, beautiful hands. The only thing that makes me stop the happiness train is when I get to his face. His face wasn't necessarily contented; it was unknowing. For someone to be happy they must know a bit of pain and I don't think Colin ever had the opportunity to know emotional distress. For some reason, this makes me a bit sad. I've always held on to the fact that Colin was never, ever unhappy, but maybe this isn't such a great event.

"So how are you today, Colinstree? Good?" He shakes his leaves at me, and I take this as an affirmation.

"You good, Colinstree?" Duet asks. She takes her plastic shovel and tries to dig at the grass beside him. I let her go for it because I know she's not strong enough to do any harm. Penelope is another story. She starts to dig at the trunk, and I crossly shoo her away.

"Why do you talk to the tree, Mommy?" she asks.

"You just talked to it, too," I reply. "Why did you?"

She thinks about this for a moment. "Well, you did first. Why did you?"

"Because this is where a part of Colin is, honey."

"Who's Colin? Why do people keep talking about him, but no one will ever tell me who he is?"

Should I? I know we have to talk about this someday. I have a script prepared in my bedroom for the occasion. I wonder briefly if I have enough time to fetch it so I can go over the highlights.

"Colin's your brother," I say gently.

"I don't have a brother."

"Well, you kind of do. You have a brother who's different than most other ones. You have one who is with you all the time."

"I don't want a brother to be with me all the time. I want you to be with me all the time."

I'm not doing this right. Orrie is going to kill me. Where do I go from here? I had this all rehearsed in my head for the blessed moment when we would have this discussion. I was to be so wise and eloquent. I have long since recognized that I can't rely on the power of ice cream forever. Treats won't keep this conversation at bay forever. In the run-through of my imagination, this all goes beautifully, like a touching vignette moment on cable television. In real life, things run awry much too quickly and easily. What do I say? *"Well, honey, you did have a brother, but something went wrong."* Will that mess her up for eternity? Will that bring her out of her comfort zone? She's so little - she's not supposed to know things don't turn out perfectly. Orrie was right. This is something we shouldn't talk about with her for another couple of years.

"Remember when you stayed with Gramma for a couple of nights?"

"No."

"It was a long time ago. Almost a year ago. You and Joanie went to a movie, remember?"

"Yeah, you and Daddy went away before Christmas."

"Yes, exactly. Well, when we went away, we went to the hospital."

"Were you hurt?"

"Yes, a little, but I'm all better now."

"Why were you at the hospital, mommy? Are you going to die?"

"Someday I will."

"No, you can't die, I'll be all alone," she whimpers as tears start to come to her eyes. I really want to stop and reassure her I'll never leave her, that I'm one of the few immortal beings around. I'm superwoman and nothing can happen to me. I want to say this but I can't.

"Don't worry, Du. I'll never leave you. Even if I die, I'll always be with you. I'll be looking down at you from Heaven. But that's not what I want to talk about."

"Why are you going to die?"

"I'm not, honey. Remember we were talking about Colin?"

"Who's Colin?"

"That's what I want to talk about."

"Is he dead? Did he die? Is he in Heaven?"

"Yes, he did. He died when Mommy was in the hospital. And yes, he's now in Heaven."

"But you didn't die."

"Nope, I'm still here."

"Do people die when they go away?"

"Sometimes."

"Will Daddy die when he's away?"

"He's pretty strong. There's no need to worry about Daddy."

"What about me, I'm little. Will I die?"

"You're the strongest little girl I know, Duet. You beat Daddy all the time when you and he arm wrestle."

"Will Penelope die? Will Kitty die? They're little."

"Kitty's pretty good at taking care of himself. He's outside all the time chasing mice. And Penelope will be with us for a long, long time."

"The mice die, don't they?"

"If Kitty is having a good night, they do."

"What do you mean?" she asks, getting teary again.

"The mice and Kitty have an agreement, so it's all okay."

"What's the agreement?"

"It's the cycle of life. It's nature."

"Does nature die?"

"Nope, it goes on forever in different forms."

"Do trees die?"

"Yep, but then other trees replace them, and the cycle goes on and on."

"What's a cycle?"

"It's part of life," I tell her.

"Are we a cycle?"

"We're part of it."

"Why did Colin die?"

"He had a neural tube defect."

"What's that? Could that happen to me?"

"Nope, that will never, ever happen to you." Thank goodness for a question that has a legitimately reassuring answer.

"Could that happen to you?"

"Nope."

"Then why did it happen to Colin?"

"Because he was a little baby, and sometimes that happens to babies."

"I'm a baby."

"No, you're a little girl."

"I'm your baby, though."

"Yes, but you're too big for that to happen. That happened while Colin was in my belly."

"Colin was in your belly?"

"Yes," I try to think of how to keep going with this conversation in a positive manner.

"I was in your belly before, did that happen to me?"

"Nope, you're right here."

"If that happened to me, would I be in the tree?"

I turn away for a second so she can't see my face. I'm about to do an ugly cry and I don't want her to see it. I want this to go well. I want to be a tower of strength for her, not a crumbling mess. I want to prove to Orrie that it's a good idea to tell Duet about Colin. If I traumatize her in any way, I'll be wrong, and I can't take that. I have to be right. I need this to be right. "It didn't happen, Du."

"Does Colin like being in the tree?"

"He's not really in the tree. Remember that I said he's now in Heaven? We just keep the tree to remember him."

"What if the wind takes away the tree?"

"The wind won't take it away."

"But if it does, would you forget him?"

"No, I'll never forget him."

"So why do you have the tree? Didn't you say you have the tree to remember him?"

I rush over to Duet and hug her. "How did you get so smart?"

"What do you mean?"

"You ask really good questions, Duet. Mommy is so proud of you."

"Do I?"

"Yep. You ask the best questions."

"I'm smart, aren't I?"

"Yes, you're brilliant."

"Yes, I am. That's why you love me."

"I love you for thirty million reasons."

"Really?"

"Yep," I profess as I swing her around and around. "I love you for all the reasons in the world."

"Do you love Colin?"

"Yes."

"Do you love me more?"

"Yes," I affirm. I'm not sure if this is the right answer. I'm not sure if it's a healthy answer. But it's the truth and I don't want to lie to her about it.

Later that evening, we're cutting up carrots for supper and Duet chirps, "I have a brother, Daddy."

"You do, do you?" Orrie asks, eyeing me suspiciously.

"Yep, he lives in a tree."

"He doesn't live in a tree, Duet," I say, avoiding Orrie's eyes.

"Well, actually," Duet reveals, trying her best to sound very grown-up, "Actually, he's dead. He's not like other brothers. He lives in Heaven."

"Is that so?" Orrie looks at me.

"Yep. He's with me all the time, just like Mommy. I love him."

"You love him?" Orrie wonders.

"Yes, he's my brother. He's special. He's not like anyone else."

Orrie gets up from the table, obviously upset. I go over to him and whisper that I'll explain later, and ask him not to be mad at me.

"I'm not angry, Avril," he says, his face all crunched up. "You can talk to Duet about Colin."

"I can?"

"Yes, of course. You can do whatever you think is best. I just didn't think it was a good idea, but obviously you felt otherwise. I don't have all the answers, you shouldn't expect me to."

"I don't think that you do ..." I start.

"Are you okay, Daddy?" Duet comes over and asks worriedly. "You're not dying, are you?"

"No, I'm fine," Orrie comforts.

"Is Mommy dying?"

"Nope."

"I just felt like I should tell her," I explain to Orrie, up high and out of Duet's earshot.

Orrie sighs heavily. "Yeah, we probably should. I don't know the right thing to do. I hate not knowing what to do. I wish there was a manual out there that explained it all."

"Me too."

He looks deeply in my eyes. "And I'm sorry if I don't talk about Colin with you. I just didn't know how to talk to you about it. I don't know what to say. I can't figure out how I feel, so how can I talk to you about it if I'm confused?"

"I'm messed up, too. I think that's okay. I think it's good to be a bit crazy in times like these. It's normal."

"Crazy is normal?" Orrie smirks.

"Totally," I smile as I give him a reassuring hug.

Duet is now jumping up and down at our feet like a baby rabbit on caffeine, trying to get in on the hug. "Are you crazy, Daddy?" she asks.

"I think so, but your Mommy is too, so it's okay."

"We're a crazy family," Duet chirps as she roars around our feet.

Orrie scoops up Duet and squeezes both of us in one huge embrace. "Yes, we are. And that's just how we like it. I wouldn't have us any other way."

CHAPTER 51

An old professor of mine, John James, has two months to live. How do you live with that realization? How did I live with the knowledge about Colin? It all seems so far away now. I have no recollection of what I went through ... it all seems so distant and foreign.

Two months.

Sixty days.

1,440 hours.

86,400 minutes.

5,184,000 seconds. 5,183,999 seconds. 5,100,000 seconds. 4,999,999 seconds.

John was one of the cool professors who hung out with the students, even though it was frowned upon by the department heads. There was never anything dodgy in the mingling. He was just incredibly interested in what his students had to say, and didn't want to imprison the discourse to the classroom. He was one of my heroes in my life's journey.

And now he dies alone. He was never married. He has no family. No brothers or sisters who live close by, or in other cities and area codes. I have no idea who will be taking care of his funeral arrangements. His secretary? Colleagues? What happens when you don't have a partner or child or parent to take care of the soiled sheets after you pass away?

I remember a picture of him that was in the lounge where the Political Sciences Society met every Thursday. He was in a field, and he was solo. He had a proud smile and a glint in his eye. Even though he looked comfortable, gratified and handsome, I always felt he looked so alone and sad. I imagined the glint in his eye hid a tear. Even though we were fairly close, I have no idea why he chose to remain single for his entire life. To the best of my knowledge, he never even dated. Did he try to date but no one would take him up on his offer? Or was he annoying and I never really knew? If you knew him beyond a close, superficial relationship, did the personality demons come out and play?

What do you think about when you're going to die? Do you try to block it out of your mind, or do you want to treasure each and every possible thought, because each and every thought could be your last? And who decides that you only have two months to live, anyway? What kind of a doctor has that knowledge? It's not like he's in a coma and is going to be pulled off life support at an assigned hour. It's not like his mother was induced and is going to deliver him to his death within a few bare hours.

When I was younger, I used to faint. A lot. Enough that it was never a shock when I woke up on the floor somewhere. I got tested for everything from diabetes to Tibetan influenza but nothing came up positive, and the doctors couldn't assess it as anything beyond a glitch in my system. It's something I've thankfully grown out of, but I remember the sensation vividly. One minute you feel a bit woozy, and then blackness caves in from the outside of your vision to the inside. After that, you spend an eternity in a state of peaceful, dreamless sleep, and then you wake up feeling refreshed, until you realize you're in a school cafeteria somewhere between the cookies and the cupcakes. I don't know whether it's in a faint that I've seen the light at the end of the tunnel, or if I've had recurring dreams about it. Maybe I've even died before. Did I die on the operating table? Whatever the case, I know what the tunnel is, and I know what the light looks like beyond it. I just have no remembrance or idea what is beyond the light.

Is this what John is wondering? Is he looking for the light? Does he believe in lights? I know he is a devoutly religious man, so he's probably unafraid of death. We actually talked about the afterlife on several occasions. When you're that secure in your immortal soul, is death welcome? Will he finally find his family after death?

I never told John about Colin. He had e-mailed a couple of times, but I never wrote back. I was going to … Is this something I should bring up? Should I tell him about my circumstances when he's in the middle of the biggest journey of his life? Would that be selfish? I go to the phone and dial the number he gave me. He's going to die in a hospital. I wonder why he doesn't want to die at home. Does he not want to leave a mess behind?

"Hello?"

"John?"

"Oh, hello, Avril. I was hoping you'd call."

"I got your message."

"I'm glad," he says in a shadow of his former voice. I wonder if I'm talking to his ghost.

"I didn't even know you were sick. No one told me."

"Really? Orrie knew. We've talked a couple of times since the diagnosis."

"What?" I screech, and then regret it. There's no need to upset John.

"Maybe Orrie forgot about it."

"Don't be foolish. This isn't something that you forget." I start to cry and try to hide it.

"So how are you doing?"

"I'm okay, you?" I blurt out before thinking.

John chuckles at the other end. "I get people with that line every time. It should be part of a psychological study."

"I feel so stupid."

"Don't."

"But I do. I just don't know what to say. I feel like I'm using up your last minutes and I'm such a waste." I'm horrified that I had the audacity to remind him these are his last minutes. I should just hang up the phone and leave him in peace.

"Don't be ridiculous. You're one of the few people I want to spend my last moments with."

"Do you want me to fly over there?" I start to blubber and I don't even try to hide it. There's no use – I'm all phlegmy and mucousy and there's no getting past it. "What do I say? I'm going to miss you. I don't know what to say," I creak.

"Just say good-bye. I just wanted to give you the chance to say good-bye."

I'm full throttle bawling now. I put the phone down and let out a couple of burping, choking sounds. "It's not fair," I get out.

"It has nothing to do with fairness."

"You're not supposed to be making me feel better, that's what I was supposed to do."

"Ah, I wasn't aware of the rules," he chides.

"Is there any chance you'll be okay?"

"No."

"I see," I respond, not knowing how else I can contribute to the conversation.

"So how are you doing? Orrie told me about what you went through."

"He did?"

"Yes, we talked quite extensively about it. I hope he's doing better; he seemed to be taking it really hard."

"He what?"

"Yes, he broke down each time we talked. He said you were the strong one who kept him going."

"He did?"

"Yes, he did."

"I never knew. He seemed very together to me."

"Maybe he didn't want you to know. He didn't want to trouble you."

"That's silly. I wanted him to be more upset. It felt like he didn't even care, sometimes."

"Well, don't be angry with him for not telling you we've talked. He must have his reasons."

"Maybe, but they're not going to be good enough."

"Promise me you'll talk to him. Think of it as my dying wish."

"Don't be crass."

"I'm just being truthful. I better go. I don't want to be rude, but I am brutally tired and need to get some rest. I've always valued your friendship, Avril. Both yours and Orrie's. I wish you the absolute best in life. I hope things go well for you and Duet and any future children you have. I'll be looking out for you."

"Thanks," I get out. "And John?"

"Yes?"

"Say hi to Colin, okay?"

John is silent for a moment and then whispers, "I would be honored to, Avril. I'll send your love."

Three weeks later, I call my mother to see if she can watch Duet for a couple of days.

"Sure, dear. What's going on?"

"We have to fly out for a funeral."

"Oh, my. Anyone I know? Whose funeral would you go to that's far enough for a plane ride? Nothing has happened to your father, has it?" I swear there is an ounce of hope in Mom's voice.

"No, no one you'd know. It was a professor Orrie and I had in university."

I hear mom washing the dishes while she's on the phone. "That seems like a lot of trouble for an old professor."

"We were both quite close to him."

She drops the phone. It makes a loud crash as it hits the floor. "Sorry about that, it slipped. And of course you were close to him. Sorry, I don't mean to pry."

"No problem, pry away. Are you sure it's no bother to look after Duet? We'll be leaving Saturday and coming home on Tuesday."

"That sounds lovely – not the funeral, of course. It would be great to have her for such a long time. I haven't had her for that long in quite a while. I –"

"No worries, Mom. I know what you mean. I'm looking forward to getting away. There's nothing wrong with that. I'm sorry that it's for a funeral, but it will be good to be on different soil for a bit."

"Yes, you will have a great time, even though I know you both don't like funerals."

I wait a bit before responding. I can tell mom is getting uncomfortable. "Who does?" I quip.

"I thought you didn't believe in funerals," she explains.

"What do you mean? That I equate them with pixies? That I don't believe in their existence? That everyone just pretends to go to them, but really they're just hanging out around old homes?"

"No, I mean that you didn't want to have a funeral for Colin."

I feel like smashing my phone on the table. Or hanging up. "That was different."

"Why? You didn't think he deserved one?"

"No, I mean that it didn't seem right," I defend. "That was a different situation. And we did have one in the end, so I don't know why you want to argue about this."

Mom's voice quivers. "I don't want to argue, Avril. I'm not even sure why I brought it up."

I throw my mother a lifesaver. "Mom, don't worry. It's fine."

"I love you, dear. I don't want to fight. I'm sorry for saying anything."

"I love you too, Mom. And so does Duet. She'll have a great time over at your place, I just know it."

"Thank you, Avie."

"For what?"

"For being such a great daughter."

"That means a lot, Mom."

"I mean it. I'm so proud of who you've become."

"Well, I better go get packed. We'll have her at your doorstep around nine o'clock. Be ready."

"I will. Love you."

"I love you too, Mom. I really do."

When I tell Duet that we're going away for a bit, she doesn't take the news well. "Are you going away forever?" she wails.

"No, sweetie. We're going away for a couple of days, and then we're coming back. You'll be with Gramma and she's really looking forward to your visit. She loves hanging out with her little monkey."

"But I'm *your* little monkey, not Gramma's."

"You're Gramma's little monkey and you're my little penguin," I correct her.

"How long are you going away for?" Duet repeats.

"A couple of days," I tell her again.

"How long is that?"

"You know how long that is, sweetie. It is three nights with the moon. Gramma will read your ABC book three different times before you go to bed. Actually, you should do some reading for Gramma to show her how well you're doing."

"Are you going to come back?"

"Of course we are. We'd never leave you. We love you too much."

"But the last time you went away it was forever."

"This time will be shorter, I promise."

"Why are you going away?"

"Because a friend of daddy's and mine died, and we're going to his funeral."

"He died?"

"Yes, he died."

"So he's dead?"

"Yes, he is."

"Is he dead like Colin?"

"Yes, he is."

"Is he going to visit Colin?"

"He said he would."

"When I die, will I see Colin?"

"I hope so, Duet."

"You don't know, though?"

"Yes, you'll see Colin. But I don't want that to happen for a long, long time."

"You don't want me to see Colin?"

"I just want you to visit his tree with me for the time being."

"What's the time being?"

"That means I want you to be with me for a long, long time."

"Mommy, I don't want you to die ever."

"Okay."

"So you won't die?"

"Well, I won't always be here on Earth, but I promise you that I'll never die."

"What do you mean?"

"That I'll be alive in Heaven."

"With Colin?"

"Yep."

"And will I be there, too?"

"Someday."

"And then we'll all be together?"

"Yep."

"How will I know Colin?"

"Because he'll look like you, only he'll be a boy."

"Then I can play with Colin, right?"

"Uh-huh."

"But you're not going to die, right?"

"Not for a long, long time."

"And you're going to come back, right? I'm not going to stay with Gramma from now on."

"No, we'll be back in four days. Can you count to four?"

"Yep, one ... two ... go!" She jumps off the bed and starts running, looking back only to see if I'm going to chase after her, which I do.

CHAPTER 52

"Orrie – I was just thinking that the last time we were away from home was when we went to the hospital about Colin."

"Yes, I suppose that's right."

We're silent for a moment, and I look around the plane for signs that it wasn't cleaned up after the last take off. Dust bunnies are a great indicator. Dust bunnies and grease spots.

"It's like we only travel for death," I whisper.

Orrie looks around to see if any of the other passengers heard me. I look at his face as he anxiously scopes the corridor to see if anyone is paying attention to his inappropriate wife.

"That's not something you should say on a plane, Avril," he whispers back. "It scares people."

"Am I scaring you?" I ask, still staring at him.

He shifts around in his seat. "No, but it makes me worried that you have thoughts like this."

"Do you ever think about Colin lately?"

"Of course I do, Avril," he says, while getting quietly, quietly angry. "I really wish you would stop talking about that right now. It's beyond annoying." He waits a minute. "Of course I think about Colin."

I look around for the food cart. "No, but sometimes it doesn't seem like you miss him. I don't want to make it sound like a competition, but sometimes it seems like I miss him a lot more than you do."

"It's not like everyone has the luxury to visibly pine all the time, Avril. Someone had to tell family about what happened. Someone had to tell friends about what happened. Someone had to go to work after everything that happened. We don't all get to spend time at home recovering. We don't all get to spend our days playing with the child that we have left. I honestly wish I had it in me to tell you to shut up."

Until this moment, I never knew that a low voice could shout so loud, and echo under my ribcage until it hurt my heart. I just never knew. I shrink back into my uncomfortable seat, hoping it would swallow me whole. I should remember to be careful for what I wish for. Until I was confronted, I believed I wanted confrontation. "I'm sorry, I never really thought about it that way."

"Shut up, Avril. Just shut up," Orrie says as he puts on his earphones and reads his book. "I don't want to talk about it."

"I'm sorry for what I said," I apologize a couple of hours later as we exit the plane.

"I still don't want to talk about it," Orrie replies.

"I think we should."

"I just want to get my luggage. Is that too much to ask?"

I try to lighten the mood. "Everyone in the plane will think we're about to have a divorce," I crookedly grin.

"Well, maybe they're not too far away from the truth."

"Oh." My heart feels physical pain from the verbal slap. I never took the time to consider the fact I was becoming unbearable. What if I lose Orrie? I can't lose Orrie after everything we've been through. He's my life. He's the father of my children. My child. He's my anchor. He's my best friend. He's –

"There's your bag," Orrie points. His voice is really gentle and has lost all traces of bitterness.

"Thank you," I blankly reply. I slowly trace a path through the people on the way to my bag. I had put a pink ribbon on the handle so I'd know it was mine, and I put a red one on Orrie's bag. Will his next wife do things like that for him? Does he have someone lined up?

"Ready?" Orrie asks.

"Yeah, I guess so."

"I didn't mean what I just said. I'm very sorry about that. I really wish I could take it back," Orrie apologizes and puts his hand on my shoulder.

"Then why did you say it? It must be on your mind on some level."

"No, it honestly isn't. It really, really isn't." He looks around. "Man, I want a coffee."

"I don't think there's anywhere close that you can get one."

"We should grab a cab and get to the hotel."

I just nod. I'm still sore from the slap, and too exhausted to say anything else. I never even considered that I was getting on Orrie's nerves. Is being annoying grounds for divorce? It scares me that I really don't have a clue what is on Orrie's mind. I've been so caught up with what I didn't believe he was thinking about, that I haven't even wondered what is on his mind. Has he been withdrawn lately? Who would get Duet if we divorced?

"Do you have the name of the hotel where we're booked?" Orrie wonders.

"No, you do. It's in your coat pocket; I put it there before we left."

"Avie, I'm sorry. I honestly didn't mean anything by what I said."

"Are you sure?"

"Yes, definitely. I couldn't exist without you."

"Me either," I cry.

"Do you want to sit down?"

"No, let's go to the hotel. If anyone asks why I'm upset, I'll just tell them we're here for a funeral."

"No one will ask."

"I know, but if they do, we have something to say."

We arrive at our hotel. After dealing with the registration, we bumble up to our room, collapsing on the bed. "I don't want to go," I whine.

"Me, either."

"Why do you think we're here?" I ask, turning towards Orrie on top of the puffy duvet.

"What do you mean?"

"I don't want to harp on the Colin subject – and please tell me if I am – but would we be here if Colin didn't die?"

"I don't follow you," Orrie slowly responds.

"Well, I really liked John. I really, really did, but I don't know if I loved him enough to jump on a plane and rearrange my life to attend his funeral. I don't even think he'd expect it."

"But we were some of the last people who he talked to," Orrie explains.

"I know, but doesn't that have more to do with the fact that he didn't have a lot of people in his life to talk to?"

"No, I think we were really close. I still don't see the connection between John and Colin, though."

"I was just thinking that if we didn't know death, then we wouldn't respect it so much. I will always miss John, but I honestly don't think that I would have gone through all of this expense to go to his funeral if we didn't go through what we did."

"I don't even know if we should be talking about this. It feels creepy."

"Talking about John, you mean?"

"Yeah, I never like to talk about a dead person until a couple of days after they die."

"Why not?"

"I don't know – it just feels safer then."

"Is that why you didn't like to talk about Colin with me?"

"No, that was for different reasons. Are you sure that you want to talk about this now?"

"I'm completely sure," I assert.

"Well, you just never seemed capable of talking about it at the first. You were so heartbroken and, I don't know ... broken, I guess. I didn't know how to approach it. You seemed like you would fall apart. And afterwards, I guess I just got so used to dealing with it on my own that I didn't want to talk about it."

"And I never respected the fact that you didn't want to talk about it. I'm sorry."

"Don't be sorry. It's good we're talking about what went on between us. But I still don't want to talk about Colin. I really, really don't. I know I will someday, but I'm not into it now. I feel like I would be just doing it to make you feel better, and that feels dishonorable to his memory. I want to talk about him when I want to talk about him. Does that make sense?"

"Not really, but that's okay," I smile.

Orrie gives me a hug and then shivers like he is shaking off droplets of water. "I'm tired," he finishes. "Let's find some coffee and get going."

We hang out at the hotel for a bit and then take a cab to the funeral. "There aren't many people here, are there?" I whisper to Orrie when we get to the proper address.

"No, not really. But I guess it makes sense. He was single, so that cuts out all of the partner's family and friends, and he didn't have any kids, so that eliminates all of his children's acquaintances, and he's been researching as opposed to teaching for a few years now, so he doesn't have any recent students. I thought there would be more of the old crew here, though," Orrie reflects as he looks around.

"People don't usually hop on a plane for a professor they hung out with over a decade ago."

"I guess," Orrie replies.

"That woman looks familiar," I point.

"Not to me," Orrie disagrees, and then we're quiet again for another ten minutes.

"Should we go to the reception afterwards?" I inquire.

"We came all this way. We should stay."

"But there's no one to talk to. I'm sure John knows we came." I nod over to the casket. "He looks weird, doesn't he?"

"Yeah. It really makes you believe in souls," Orrie ponders. "It's so apparent when you look at a corpse that the physical body is nothing more than a vessel. He looks so fake."

"Yeah, he definitely looks empty," I agree.

"When I was a kid and my guinea pig died, I remember thinking that animals just look like they're sleeping when they're dead. Even when we were burying her, I kept thinking she would open her eyes and wiggle out of the dirt. It's never like that with humans. When humans die, they look like a deflated balloon. It's like the life force is some sort of spiritual air pump that keeps you going, and once it's gone, the body just sinks into its bones. Nothing that was, is truly left."

"Ashes to ashes and all that," I sigh.

"Yeah, the spirit goes to God and the body goes to mother nature."

"So do you see God as a man?" I wonder.

"I guess I do. I guess that my first image of God was as a man, so it became ingrained in my mind."

I wait a few minutes and ask, "What did Colin look like after he died?"

"Funny, I was just thinking of that." Orrie pauses for a moment, and I assume he's reflecting on using the word *funny* when speaking about this. "He looked the same as when he was alive."

"So do you think he was too young to have a spirit?"

"Not at all. I just don't think I knew him well enough to tell the difference."

"That's pretty depressing," I frown.

"The whole situation is sad, Avie. The only thing that isn't is that we've kept going and it hasn't broken us."

"I feel a little broken sometimes."

"I think that's a good sign. Feeling a little broken is healthy. Being broken is different."

After the funeral, we are directed downstairs for a remembrance gathering. We chat with John's secretary for a few minutes, but she's the only person we know, and we don't really know her at all. "Should we go now?" I ask, after what I deem an appropriate amount of time.

Orrie looks around. "Yeah, I guess so."

"I feel like a ghost, sometimes." I say out of the blue as we get to the coat rack.

"Why?"

"I don't know, I just do. Or at least I did. I think I'm getting over it."

Orrie helps me put on my jacket. "Come on, let's get something to eat."

I try to be respectfully despondent over dinner, but when I think of John's body, I remember it as being so alien, I can't muster up the emotion. For some reason, knowing he's not here – not really – makes me feel better. I wonder if John has said "hi" to Colin yet. I envision them talking, and by the time I get to dessert, I know things are going to be okay. I don't know why, I just do. Nothing like death to make you realize you're really alive. Thanks, John. Not sure if this was your final intention, but it worked, nonetheless.

"Do you want a bite of my sandwich?" Orrie asks on the flight home.

"No thanks."

"Why? Aren't you hungry?"

"No, my stomach is a bit queasy. I might just stick to the crackers."

"Are you still upset?"

"No, I feel fine, just too much food last night," I laugh as I lean over and kiss his cheek. "I feel better than I have in a long time."

Orrie sits back in his chair, contented. "I'm glad we worked things out. I guess I got too caught up in the belief that it's not good to fight. I kept things inside that we should have had a nice brawl over. I'm going to work on that," he smiles.

"Do you remember when Duet was little and she used to say "achoo" for "I love you"? We couldn't figure out what she was saying for the longest time because everything else that she said was mimicked from us. This was the only phrase she had of her own, so it took a bit of detective work to determine what she meant."

"Yeah, I remember."

"Orrie – achoo."

"Achoo too, Avie. I really, really do."

CHAPTER 53

Dear God,

I'm back. Or at least mostly. I'm sorry for ignoring you. I just needed some space. I needed some time to figure this out for myself, and for a while there, I didn't trust you for guidance. Sorry about that. I'm not meaning to be rude, I'm just being honest. I sincerely hope that isn't an unforgivable thing for me to say to you. No use trying to lie to you, anyway. Apparently you can hear my thoughts even before I have them, so I might as well exhibit full disclosure.

It's going to take some time before we're back to where we were. I can only hope you're okay with that. I'm finding myself talking to you a little bit more and more each day. I'm not sure if I've ever really stopped our conversations entirely. I'm sure they've subconsciously continued in the back reaches of my psyche, but now it's full-on and open. I realize that you weren't ignoring me. Sometimes we ask for things, and the answer is no.

I know I missed out on a lot of comfort by not depending on you. Maybe I was subconsciously punishing myself by not leaning on you for support. Or maybe I was just angry. Either way, I know it's my loss to be separated from you for any reason. I have to keep reminding myself that your role isn't to take the pain away all of the time; it is to help deal with the pain when it comes.

I want you to tell me everything is going to be okay. I need to feel that from you. But I know that can't happen, and it never could. I guess what I need most, is to not be afraid of that. Can I pray for that? Is that a prayer that can be answered?

And I thank you that I'm getting better. I'm really sure I'm on my way.

– Avril

CHAPTER 54

"So when do you want to start telling people? Do you want to wait until the ultrasound this time?"

"I don't know," I reply, still dazedly looking at the stick in my hand. "I don't think I want to wait too long. This is big news."

"True. But maybe we should err on the side of caution," Orrie considers, while leaning on the door frame.

"I don't want to go through this pregnancy with the fear that something is going to go wrong. Something very right has happened – I'm pregnant – and I want to go into this with a fresh perspective. I'm not going to worry about every single body twitch. It's not good for the baby's morale."

"Yes, that's probably best. Are you excited?" Orrie asks.

"Yes, are you?"

Orrie beams. "Very."

"Do you think of this baby as a replacement for Colin?"

"No, do you?"

"No, not at all. I just wanted to check that you didn't either. This baby is its own entity. If Colin was still alive, we'd have three kids to play in the front yard," I reflect. "Now, we'll just have two."

"I'm so excited," Orrie repeats. "It's going to be a lot of fun having another baby around. Of course, this means you probably won't return to work for another while yet."

"I can only assume you mean paid work, right? There will be lots of work to be done around here with two kids," I chide. "And, yes – staying home with two kids suits me just fine." Just fine, indeed.

Later that night, I sit on the deck drinking hot peppermint tea, hanging out with my favourite star. He's shining brightly tonight. I look down in the yard at Colin's tree. The moonlight shimmers on each of the tiny leaves, making it appear to be dancing in the night. I sit back in my chair, feeling reflective. Life is circular. There are no beginnings and endings in life, just differing rotations. Birth isn't the beginning and death isn't the end – it just keeps going and rolling while constantly changing. I think it's like pushing a tire on the surf at the beach. A dry tire picks up a bit of sand. It rolls into a tidal pool where it gets all wet and salty. Then it gets all mucky and muddy when you push it past the wet sand, and eventually it gets all chunky and doughy when it reaches the hot sand. Ultimately, it gets dry again, so all the sandy bits flake off and you're back to a black tire that's aching to return to the ocean. A rolling tire is constant, but looks different because of the situations it finds itself. And sometimes the tire falls flat, making it dependent on someone else to push it and start the cycle again.

Life is always going round and round, but that doesn't mean it ever stays the same. It just means we create false starts and pretend things have an ending. Chapters never close on life because no one's reading about it. It just happens.

Does this make sense, Baby? I hope so. I want you to know I'm not afraid to love and adore you. I'm ecstatic you're beginning this particular journey with me. You're going to have a great time with me. I hope you enjoy the ride. It's always interesting. And I mean that in the best way possible.

ABOUT THE AUTHOR

Michelle Harris-Genge lives deep in the woods of beautiful Prince Edward Island with her husband and two amazing children.

Michelle had been writing in her work-world forever, but only recently plunged into the realm of sharing her creative writing. Michelle keeps busy co-writing *The Terra Obscura Chronicles* with her husband, Geoff. This is her first solo effort. Michelle also writes the pause2effect blog online.

Michelle enjoys biking, skiing and finding new keto desserts. She is hoping to get a gym membership soon. Her body isn't pleased with being scrunched over a computer screen for entire days on end and is starting to revolt.

Made in the USA
San Bernardino, CA
27 July 2019